A CATERPILLAR IS WAITING

*God has a plan for you. Yes! A master plan!
Just wait and see.*

Uma Ramachandran

PARTRIDGE

A Penguin Random House Company

To order additional copies of this book, contact
Partridge India
000 800 10062 62
orders.india@partridgepublishing.com

www.partridgepublishing.com/india

Contents

Dear friends,

Do you ever feel, "What can I do? What difference can I make? I am just an ordinary person?" No. Those who have read this book are no longer ordinary. You are extra-ordinary. Your life is not a matter of chance or accident. God has a plan for you, a master plan! Yes. ***You are the light of the world!***

The world needs young
And steady hands
To guide it right today
Be it yours
To lead the way.

Hold high the torch
In your strong hands
The future lies today
Hold high your torch
Its light may help
Others on the way.

Whatever dreams you're dreaming
May each one of them come true
Whatever plans you're making
May they all work out for you
And may you have more happiness
Than only words can tell.
Not only as the years begin
But in the days that follow as well
So here with deep affection
Is a wish for all life through
That everything you want the most
Will find its way to you.

I extend my good wishes to all the readers of this book.

Dedication

The good qualities and discipline that are taught early in our lives, in school and college, make an indelible impression on our minds and enable us to progress in life. I therefore dedicate this book to all my teachers (who groomed me into what I am today) in Church Park Convent, St. Ignatius Convent, and Fatima College.

"A good teacher is worth a million books."

—Author

Foreword

From time immemorial, the existence of a God has always been a controversial issue. The author has dealt with this subject very interestingly and at the same time, very clearly, making use of scientific truths and observations.

In this turbulent 21st century torn asunder with war and strife, this book comes like a breath of fresh air and soothes and elevates the mind to unknown heights. Interspersed with interesting anecdotes it has a gripping style which touches your very core. It is a must for the youth and not only for the youth-it is a book for all ages and all times-a book that would illumine one from within and change ones very own existence. The author has attempted to remove all the misconceptions from the minds of the people and replace them with healthy ideas.

This book explains many ideas which are of great relevance to people of all countries. It will not be an exaggeration to say that this book is a treasure—house of knowledge which everyone should acquire and share with others.

I extend my best wishes to the author and pray that her good work continues.

—Prajapathy

Preface

Dear friends! This is a competitive world. Everyone wants to win the race. You have to face this competition and make a mark for yourself. You may have to cross many a hurdle and solve many a problem. This book will help you battle against the odds in life and march towards victory.

A brilliant future awaits you. You should not rest content with your victory over others. You should defeat yourself. In other words, you should expose the hidden power in you. That is called the 'Excel yourself theory'. Accept the fact that in certain ways you are unique.

At the same time, you should be able to take others also with you on the ladder of success. If you follow what is said in this book, you will see that your life—every minute of it—is transformed almost magically.

Many people have several doubts about God. With science as basis, this book answers the most important questions you will ever ask.

Every science subject has its own principles governing it. In the same manner, spirituality also has its own principles. The great universal laws of nature are the laws of spirituality and we must know that every religion preaches us the laws of nature. Religion is pure science.

Man is constantly abusing the great laws of nature through wrong thinking, which leads to his own destruction. This ignorance is the root cause for all evil conditions. We have to obey nature. There is no other choice. Today the whole world is afflicted by militancy and violence. All the countries are trying to find out ways of combating this evil in vain. The solution is very simple and it is given in this book.

A single thought can change the world, because a good thought comes from the soul which is the seat of God. Nothing is impossible. Our hearts are beads and Divine love is the thread that will hold in a garland of unity. Let us resolve, this very moment to become members of one large family.

—Author

1

Life is short

Here is an interesting story about time. In a certain village there was a man who was always thinking of death with fear and anxiety. Hence, he sat in penance and worshipped Lord Yama. In due course, the Lord appeared before him and asked him what he wanted. The man replied, "My Lord, I am terribly scared of death. It also saddens me. Hence do not take me away suddenly. Warn me three times at least, and then take me, so that I'll be prepared." The Lord granted his wish and vanished.

Years passed. One day, Lord Yama appeared before the man and said, "Your life span is over. Come with me." The man was shocked. Greatly perturbed, he said, "What is this? I had asked you to warn me three times. You have not done so. You have broken your promise." Lord Yama replied calmly, "How can you say that I have not warned you? I gave you grey hairs. That was the first warning. Then your head became bald. That was the second warning. Then your skin developed wrinkles. That was the third warning. If you didn't heed all these warnings, I'm not responsible. The past is past. It will never return. Now come with me."

When I see the photographs taken when I was a college student, it seems as if just a day has passed. But now my children have completed their college studies. Very soon, my grand-children too would have become graduates. Yes. Life is short and fleeting. We must use it well. That is my objective in writing this book.

2

The story of a village boy

All of as have a lot of problems in life, and we certainly have to face them. At the same time we have several duties to fulfill towards our country and our people. Sometimes when problems keep mounting one over the other, worry and fear grips us and we wonder how we are going to surmount them.

Depression eats the very core of our being and havocs like a canker. A depressed man radiates only unpleasant and morbid vibrations all around. Here is a little story which shows us how we can behave in such circumstances and tackle our problems.

A village boy was sitting under a tree with a lantern in his hand. He had to go to the next village which was six miles away. Since it had become very dark, he dreaded the journey and sat under the tree with a fearful heart. An old man who came along looked at the boy and asked, "Why are you sitting alone under a tree with a lantern in your hand?"

The boy answered, "I have to travel six miles in this darkness, but the light from this lantern shines for only about three feet. Hence I do not know how to travel the six miles."

The old man laughed and said, "You are going to walk with the lantern in your hand. As you walk, the light which shines from the lamp will come with you. With the aid of that, if you travel three feet, you will have the light from the lantern for the 'next three feet'. In this way, with the help of your lantern, you could travel not only six miles, but countless number of miles."

It was then that the little boy realised an important truth. Even if the light from the lantern shorn for only three feet, since he took it along with him, he could get light from it 'continuously'. Once he understood this he began walking with renewed hope and courage in his heart

In the same way, man's power is limited because our conscious mind is limited in its concepts by the five physical senses which testify only to what we see, hear, taste, touch and smell. But God dwells within us. So if we unite our limited power with that of the Almighty, **on a permanent basis,** we could overcome any kind of problem and reach our goal successfully. Christ says, "The Kingdom of God lies within", and all other religions agree with Him.

It is enough to remember that we are not alone without any strength. God is here within us, beside us and around as. We are not a dry twig but a living fruitful branch. We are born to win and succeed. Let us move upward, onward and Godward. I have given several messages and tips that would prove to be a turning point in your lives.

3

Personality

All of us represent a unique value in the universe because our personality and individuality is unlike that of any other human being who has ever lived and who will ever live. We don't have any exact duplicates. This is because each human soul is distinct and different.

We are not our physical body. Our body is just an 'outer garment' which is liable to decay during death. But our real self is our soul and because of it we have identy, individuality, personality, essential intelligence and ego. In other words our soul is actually the seat of all that we really are. It contains our entire intelligence both bestowed and acquired.

Some think that the brain creates thoughts. The human brain does not contain thought or create thought. It simply responds to thought. It delivers thoughts. The brain is an electro-chemical machine. Intelligence is resident in the soul. The soul acts upon its instrument, the brain. The brain then translates these impulses into ideas, words, and action.

We have seen that the power of the soul is unlimited because it is a part of God. How are we going to use this power? We must know things in their proper light.

The soul rejects negative thoughts like anger, hatred, jealousy and selfishness. So these destructive emotions find an outlet and are expressed as ulcers, heart trouble, tension etc.. So we ruin ourselves by our wrong attitude. Hence they must be entirely rooted out.

Like attracts like. This is a great law. Divine qualities like love, peace and patience increases the potentialities of the soul. So the more we attune ourselves to it and make use of it the more we succeed in life.

Man is born of free will. We have been left to work out our destiny. The happiest man is he who brings forth the highest and the best in him. So once again I repeat—let us move upward, onward, and Godward. Life is self renewing. A stream can never go backward.

4

The story of Vyasa

We have learnt that saints were able to perform miracles. Saints were not born with a silver spoon. All the great personages in sacred history were men of tremendous faith in their spiritual power of the soul, in their divine heritage.

There is a difference between faith and belief. Belief is superficial and easily shaken, but faith makes us strong and steadfast.

A great sage, Vyasa, was seated on the bank of the Jamuna when some gopis come on their way to visit Lord Krishna. There was no ferry and they were eager to cross the river. So they asked Vyasa if he could carry them across. "Yes, but I am very hungry. First give me something to eat", Vyasa replied. The gopies laid their offerings before him and Vyasa ate them all. With anxiety they watched him and then asked again how they should cross.

Vyasa stood by the river and said "O Jamuna! As I have eaten nothing today, so do thou divide thy waters and let these gopies pass over." The gopies listened in wonder, remembering all that he had eaten. But the waters were divided and they crossed over. Vyasa had tremendous faith in his spiritual power. He did not attach any importance to his physical body. He knew that his soul was above all physical needs; and it was of this nature alone that he was conscious when he spoke.

5

Can we trust quack astrologers?

When beset by a string of misfortunes, some people seek the advice of astrologers. Only a few astrologers are proficient enough to guide people properly and avert impending disasters. The majority of them merely try to exploit people's ignorance and extort money, without really being proficient in the art of predicting.

In reality, astrology is a unique art and those who are well-versed in it, can predict future events with great precision. For example, an astrologer foretold that Caesar would die on 15th March. On the morning of the fateful day, Caesar called the astrologer and said arrogantly, "You said I would die on 15th March. But I'm still alive." The astrologer replied, "Yes, my lord; 15th March has dawned, but it has not set yet." True enough, that very day Caesar was murdered by his own friends.

Today, however, many fake astrologers and so-called saints are deceiving the people and amassing wealth without any strain. An acquaintance of mine was suffering from chronic headache. She went to an astrologer. Under the pretext of curing her, he took hold of her hair and kept swinging her head for more than an hour. As a result, her whole head became swollen and her headache increased. She had also to part with a lot of money as fees to the astrologer.

The important point to remember about this incident is, that it is the simple uneducated people who are easily deceived by these fake astrologers. It is better to communicate directly with God and seek redress to our problems than depend on such middlemen.

Some people also believe that wearing certain 'lucky' rings will solve all their problems. This will only lead to loss of money. After you have read this book, you will realise very clearly, ways of solving your problems. The fundamental teaching of the Bhagavat Gita is "Don't worry". One who knows the majesty of his own soul never loses his courage or faith.

6

Lucky dress

Many college students have a particular dress to be worn for the examinations. They will only wear that dress for all the examinations. They firmly believe that that dress will help them to get high marks in the examination. How ridiculous! If they do not study and wear that dress, will they get good marks? In the midst of great scientific and technological advancement, in the 21st century, how does such a superstition survive? Dear students, trust your ability. Trust your hard work. Above all, trust your own self.

There are some merchants who have the picture of an ass in their shops. Every morning, they worship that picture and then only start the day's work. They believe that this will increase their business. The truth is, those who sell the asses' pictures make a lot of money.

Many good people, when they are beset with suffering, tend to lose faith in God. This is because we fail to realise the true dimensions of life. For example, let us imagine that a man commits a murder. The incident does not end there. The victim (of the murder) suffers immense agony before he dies. His wife and children also suffer, perhaps all their lives, due to the death of the head of the family. Nature sees to it that the murderer experiences the same kind of suffering that these people have experienced. If one lifetime is not sufficient, it continues in the next birth also.

Thus all of us have to reap the rewards or punishment for all our actions. We cannot be impatient to be rid of them. We have a long way to go. Truly has Robert Frost said, "I have miles to go before I sleep."

Many of us lose faith in God because we expect instant results. Let us hear what Lord Krishna says. "Mind your own daily business. The fruit will come by itself. The business is with the action only, never with its fruits." We must have the patience to wait for the cosmic law to work out. Remember Rome was not built in a day.

Full scheme of life

Having come from God, our ultimate destination is also God. Just as the water sucked up from the ocean descends as rain and once again reaches the ocean, the journey of our life will not end till we reach God. We have no choice in this. We cannot break the journey in the middle. Life is full of meaning and purpose. Let us understand the full scheme of life. There is no short cut to God. Only those who have lived a righteous life can reach God easily.

What is religion?

Religion means 'reunion with God'. 'ligion' means union. So re+ligion is reunion. All religions advocate a clean and righteous life as a means to reach God. But problems arise when people who know nothing of their religion set certain principles for themselves and try to follow them. Considering these facts, the entire system of our education, religious thinking, moral training and daily living, will have to be drastically changed.

Remember, that

1. God is not in any one place, but everywhere.
2. We are not alone in the battle of our life.
3. We have a power greater than all the odds against us, constantly by our side.

> *"It is better to understand a little*
> *than to misunderstand a lot."*

Some people condemn religion without knowing anything about it. They think themselves very clever. The Katha-Upanishad says of these, "Fools dwelling in ignorance, yet imagining themselves wise and learned . . ."

A little learning is a dangerous thing. Spiritual truth has been disfigured. God has been portrayed as a magician. Tear the veil of such ignorance. In ancient times the "Gurukula" system of education prevailed. This system included spiritual education. Society then was good. But now superstition destroys the entire social fabric resulting in war and all kinds of hideous conditions. Readers must now pause for a moment and think what can be done now. The alarm bell has rung. A new intelligent force is needed now in this world. Are we handicapped? The Allaudhin lamp is with us. Our ancestors have provided us with a rich culture and civilization.

7

We are one

I would like to begin with a reference to a unique Indian festival. It gives me a great pleasure and a sense of pride to write about this.

The festival is called 'RAKSHA BANDHAN'. It is celebrated every year in August. Rakhi originated in Rajasthan. People of all religions gather together; and the ladies tie the 'rakhi' on the hands of men. Thenceforth, the men are considered to be their brothers by the ladies. After the rakhi is tied, the sister honours the brother with gifts, and there is a feast. The brother in turn, gives her money. Thus an everlasting bond is established between two total strangers. Cultivation of a feeling of brotherhood among members of different communities, is the main objective of this festival

There have been instances of even enemies being transformed into friends by the bond of the rakhi. In times of war, women who received information that their husbands would be killed by the enemy king, would send him a rakhi. The king, who thus became the 'brother' of the said lady, desisted from killing his 'brother-in-law' and instead helped his new sister. Even large-scale wars have been brought to an end in this manner. What a unique relationship!

Rakhis were tied to the British agents too (when they were here) by many Indian women. The British in turn, have given due respect to the sentiments attached to the rakhi.

In this context, I would like to narrate an incident that took place in my own life. We were on a visit to one of my relatives living in another town. As it was our first visit, we wanted to ask somebody for directions. Unfortunately, there was no one in sight, expect a man who made a living by climbing palm trees and plucking the fruits. He was walking a little ahead of us. So I called out to him as brother, "Brother, please wait a minute." He merely turned back and thinking that I had called someone else, went on his way. His station in life being much lower than ours, he did not expect me to call out to him. However, when I repeated my call, he turned and asked, "Did you call me?" When I said "Yes" his face lit up like a thousand watt bulb. He was thrilled that I had called him 'brother'. On my request for directions, he obliged by escorting us right up to my relatives' house. I have had this experience not once, but several times—of people rejoicing at being shown sisterly affection.

Swami Vivekananda had gone to America to attend the International Convention of World Religions. All the speakers began their speeches with the words, "Ladies and Gentlemen". Vivekananda alone, began his speech with the words, "Sisters and Brothers". The audience was immensely pleased and there was thunderous applause. It is this love and affection that can transcend national and religious barriers and unite men and women. It can be called divine love. Don't we say, Love is God? It is this feeling of brotherhood that can annihilate all differences and pave the way for universal peace.

Global Village:

Today, the progress of science has enabled the people of the world to come closer. Geographical barriers have been broken and the world has shrunk into a global village.

> *"Our phases are different, our faces are different, our races are different,*
> *So what? We are all children of God*
> *In that one single breath of life, we are connected.*
> *WE ARE ONE!"*

Our hearts are the beads and divine love is the thread that will hold them together in a garland of unity.

Let us resolve, this very minute, to become members of one large family by tying the rakhi. Let the whole world celebrate Raksha Bandhan. I extend my good wishes to all the readers of this book.

8

The story of the Parrot

A parrot which is confined to a cage, beats its wings and tries to fly. The man who imprisoned the parrot cuts off its wings. The parrot resigns itself to its fate helplessly. As the wings grow, the man cuts them again. If this is done three or four times, the parrot gives up the effort to fly. Even if the cage is opened and it is released, it returns to the cage. What is worse, it believes that the cage is its permanent home. We should never become like the parrot. We should never give up our efforts. Perseverance will always lead to success.

"It is your attitude, not your aptitude that determines your altitude." We reap what we sow. Life is like a bank account. We get only what we put in.

We can compare God to a teacher. Only if a student studies well and writes the examination well, can the teacher give him good marks. God is in the same position. He can reward only the good.

"Our greatest glory is not in never falling, but in rising every time we fall."

—*Oliver Goldsmith.*

9

The story told by Vivekananda

Swami Vivekananda explained our present-day situation through a story. A lioness which went hunting, delivered a cub and died. A herd of sheep which happened to pass by, took pity on the lion's cub and took it into its fold. The cub considered itself as a sheep, drank sheep's milk, ate grass and was as meek as a lamb. At this time, a lion came there. Observing the cub behaving like a lamb, the lion was shocked and enraged. It caught the cub by its neck. The cub was scared and pleaded, "Please leave me. I am a harmless innocent lamb." But the lion said, "You are not a lamb. You are a lion that can overthrow even an elephant. You are the king of the forest." The cub was very confused. The lion took the cub to a well and asked it to look at its reflection in the water. "Look at your true self. Are you a lamb? Look at your majesty." So saying the lion roared, sending a tremor through the whole forest. That very instant, the cub also realised that it was not a lamb. It roared majestically.

Many of us are like the lion's cub in the story. We fail to recognize our strength, knowledge, love, beauty, wisdom, truth, majesty and worth, and live as if devoid of all these. In truth, all of us possess these treasures. It is the dirt surrounding our soul or essence that prevents us from realising our own worth and strength. All the mistakes committed by us knowingly or otherwise, remain as seeds in our sub-conscious mind. This is called the cosmic record. It is these seeds (dirt) which are responsible for our sorrows. A pure soul is very powerful. How can we rid ourselves of this dirt? By meditating for a specific period everyday. In course of time, we can feel our happiness and wisdom increasing. "Knowing oneself is the foundation stone of knowledge." We can realise our hidden power only through meditation.

In this context, I wish to state an important truth. Lord Jesus and Lord Buddha were empowered to perform miracles and reveal the truths about life, only after meditating for several years. We should not forget this. Lord Jesus was missing for eighteen years. Buddha went into seclusion for eight years. We must purify our soul amidst our daily activities

10

Leaders are not born

No one is born a saint in this world. They are made saints. For example, Mahatma Gandhi. With love as his only weapon, he won freedom for our country, and is honoured by the whole world today. Martin Luther King, who won liberty for the negro slaves, encountered defeat in his initial attempts. He then came to India, stayed here for a month, observed Gandhi's practice of Ahimsa, returned invigorated and then succeeded in his mission.

Gandhi himself has recorded in his autobiography, that he was an average man. When his father was ill, Gandhi was happy with his wife, ignoring his father. It was only after seeing the play "Harichandra" that he resolved never to utter falsehood, practised meditation everyday and became a Mahatma. Is it easy to lead thirty crore people? How did Gandhi the man acquire this power? Only through meditation. Prayer links God's power with our efforts.

Take another example—Swami Vivekananda. He was not sure whether God existed or not. He asked several people this question, but did not receive a satisfactory answer. It was only after he met Sri. Ramakrishna Paramahamsa that his doubts were dispelled. Even so, because his family was very poor, he asked Sri.Ramakrishna to pray for the betterment of his family. The latter refused. Once again, Vivekananda lost his faith in God. Later he practised meditation himself, gained enlightenment, and then travelled across the world, spreading the light of his knowledge.

As we meditate, our mind becomes purer and purer. A pure soul is very powerful. This applies even to inanimate objects. For example, iron is refined to such an extent that it becomes almost equal to silver. This is possible because God lives even in these objects. Higher forms of energy do not dwell only in our body. Our mind is the medium through which we can realise God. Our youngsters should understand this and come forward to work for the betterment of our nation. Everybody can become a leader.

> *"The world needs young*
> *And steady hands.*
> *To guide it right today*
> *Be it yours*
> *To lead the way*
> *Yes! You are the light of the world."*

Divine heritage

Let us believe in our divine heritage. Let us remind ourselves constantly that we are the children of God, that our life is not a matter of chance or accident, but that we have come directly from that one unchanging source. Some men have firm faith in their physical strength; others in their intellectual power. But the truly strong man is he who has faith in his spiritual nature. Let us have faith in our soul which is immortal and unalterable, rather than in fleeting and material things. We must know that God is very close to us. He is our innermost being, the Soul of our soul, the Life of our life, and the very foundation of our being.

Jesus

Jesus could heal the sick, awaken the dead, and turn water into wine. How was he able to do this? He said, "I and my Father are one." Those who are one with God can perform miracles. "Know ye not that ye are the temple of God, and that the spirit of God dwelleth in thee?" If we can purify and expand our mind through mediation, and receive God in our consciousness, we too can do wonders.

11

The scientist of all scientists

Who are we? Where did we come from? Which came first—the egg or the hen? These are questions that we have been asking for long. We are eager to find the answer to these questions. Let us consider a scientific truth.

According to scientists, we cannot create or manufacture a new species of living beings. But God created man without any raw materials; He created trees without any seeds. Let us see the various living creatures (besides man) that God has created:

Invertebrate	1,28,000	types
Insects	9,50,000	"
Crabs	25,000	"
Fishes	30,000	"
Amphibians	3,000	"
Reptiles	6,000	"
Birds	8,950	"
Mammals	4,500	"

Scientists have discovered all these species.

God is omnipotent, possessed of all virtues and the source of all light. Man, whom God created in his image, was also like God. But because of his ignorance, desire and selfishness, man lost his divinity, committed evil deeds, underwent suffering and belittled himself. Like the lion's club in the story, we should realize that we are not lambs any more. Religions are instruments that serve to bring out the divinity in us. So, instead of letting time and fate overcome us, let us shape our destiny by following the path of righteousness. Life is self renewing.

The scientist for all scientists

Scientists may say that they have invented this or that. But they have not really invented anything. They have only uncovered what was already there: the vibratory blueprint hidden in the ether. God alone is the scientist of all scientists.

Also vibrating in the ether are the concepts for every invention that man has made or will make in the future. These vibrations are all around us, and there is a method of contacting them directly. That method is through the all-knowing intuitive power of the soul.

Great souls who reveal deep spiritual truths to mankind, receive their knowledge through direct attunement with the vibrations of those truths, and hence we can rely upon them.

Origin

We have now understood all about our origin and what we are made of. Let us realize the majesty of our soul. Let us have faith in our divine nature and follow the path of righteousness.

> Infinity I am
> All light I am
> All joy I am
> All glory I am
> All knowledge I am.

Let us not demean ourselves by thought, word or deed.

In Science

We learn about sound waves, light waves, electric waves and the power of gravity through science. But the power of our soul is greater than the power of all these. The power of our soul is unlimited.

A Caterpillar

A caterpillar is waiting in each one of us, to become a butterfly. The power of our soul is hidden in us. Some of us have recognized our inner self. Let all of us unfold the occult powers hidden within us by realizing and understanding the power of our soul. We suffer on this earth due to our lack of soul development.

12

Where is God?

Many of us search for God. A small story, I think, will serve to explain this. A merchant was traveling by train to a distant place, with a lot of money. In his compartment, there was only one fellow passenger. The merchant was very cautious, as he was afraid that his fellow passenger might rob him of his money. As the train neared his destination, the merchant wanted to check if his money was safe. He looked through all his belongings but could not find the money. He was terribly upset and depressed. He looked at his fellow passenger with suspicion. He was sure that the man was the thief. His companion understood the meaning of the merchant's look. But he remained unperturbed. He was not guilty, and so he sat calmly, smiling at the merchant.

After a while, seeing the merchant's distress, the fellow passenger asked him, "What are you searching for?" "I can't find my money", said the merchant. The fellow traveler said, "There are only two of us here. Please look through your belongings slowly and calmly." The merchant did as he was told and found that his money was quite safe.

Many of us are like the merchant in the story. Without realizing God's presence within ourselves, we search for Him outside. That is why we cannot find him. If we build a beautiful house, and fill it with garbage, who will visit us? In the same manner, we can see God only if we have a pure mind.

Show me God

Many people have said to me, "If you believe that there is a God above, show Him to us." Many saints have seen God in person. But even they, have seen God only after they conditioned themselves to see God. All of us cannot become doctors. One has to study the specified subject for a specified period. But all of us can see God. In fact, we are all marching towards that goal. But unless we follow the path of righteousness we shall not reach the goal. We must conquer all our lower propensities and realize our higher self. We have to follow a practical method; every religion offers us that method. We can certainly see God, but only after we have rid our souls of all stains. We should remember that those who sin are moving far away from God.

Ghee in Milk

We get ghee only from milk. But it is hidden in milk. Similarly, though we cannot see God, we can feel his presence. When we meditate on God sincerely, tears begin to flow from our eyes. Those tears are testimony to the presence of God. God lives in every atom of his creation. A simple person, full of faith, full of devotion and full of sincerity, knows a great deal about God.

13

Saint Ramanujar

Once upon a time, there lived a saint called Ramanujar. He studied the Scriptures under a guru (teacher). When the time came for him to leave, (the school) his Guru taught him a mantra, and told him that if he chanted the mantra everyday sincerely, he would attain salvation. He also said that Ramanujar was not to utter the mantra to anybody else; if he did so, he would go to hell.

Ramanujar, however disobeyed his Guru's orders. He went into a temple and said to the devotees assembled there, "All those who wish to attain salvation, come here." The people gathered round him. He then taught them the mantra that his guru had taught him. When the guru came to know of this, he was shocked. He summoned Ramanujar and asked him, "I had told you that if you revealed this mantra to anyone, you would go to hell. Why did you tell everyone the mantra?" Ramanujar replied, "If a hundred people can go to heaven by my going to hell, I think it is a small price. But please pardon me for disobeying your orders."

The guru was overwhelmed by Ramanujar's magnanimity, and embraced him saying that Ramanujar was much greater than himself. From this we learn that leading others in the path of righteousness is a very virtuous act. Readers of this book! Please share these views with your friends and earn the blessings of God. Let us spread the light of knowledge and dispel the darkness of ignorance.

"Hold high the torch
In your strong hands;
The future lies today
Hold high your torch
Its light may help
Others on the way"

14

The fruits that God ate

Once there lived a merchant. He had resolved to offer 200 bananas to God. He gave 200 bananas to his servant and asked him to hand them over to the temple authorities. But he did not give the servant any money or food to be taken on the way to the temple. Poor servant! he felt hungry on the way. So he took four bananas from the bunch and ate them. He gave the remaining 196 bananas to the temple authorities and returned home. That very night God appeared in the merchant's dream and asked. "You promised to give me 200 fruits, but I received only four. Where are the remaining 196?" The merchant realized his mistake. God resides in every living being, in the form of a light. Hence, the good that we do to any living being reaches God. According to the Christian code of conduct, kindness to God's creatures reaches His mighty throne sooner than anything else on earth. At the same time, when we are sinning against any living being, we are sinning against God.

"They alone live who live for others. The rest are more dead them alive."

"He who giveth to the poor lendeth to the Lord."

Even if we feed a dog, it is equal to feeding God. That is why Indians laid down charity as the basis of all their day-to-day activities. As soon as cooking is over, it is a practice in India to offer a ladle full of rice to the crows. Women use rice flour to put kolams in front of their houses. Ants and other small creatures eat the rice flour in the kolams. Indians laid greater emphasis on social work than on individual advancement.

Let us study a chapter from the great epic Silappathigaram. Kovalan and Kannagi are husband and wife. But soon after their marriage, Kovalan leaves his wife for another lady called Madhavi. Kannagi wilts in solitude. Later, Kovalan leaves Madhavi and returns to Kannagi. But she does not chide him and say, "Why did you desert me? All my youth is wasted." On the other hand, she was distressed that, devoid of his income, she was unable to help the poor with money. Seeing her distress, his parents were also distressed. So she asked Kovalan, "Was it proper on your part to make your aged parents sad?" Literature is the reflection of life. The epic Silappathigaram reveals the fact that people in those days placed great value on common good. That is the way to reach God. Even if we dress ourselves in gorgeous silks and dine in five star hotels, all that extravagance does not enter into our account. But if we give just ten rupees to a poor man, it is entered in our credit and returned to us.

A girl called Annam worked as a servant in our house. When she first came she was very slim. After a few days' stay in our house, she became plump. Being fatherless, she said, they were very poor. Her mother worked in the fields and brought up five children with great difficulty. The story of her life was quite moving. When her mother started cooking, the children would rush to the kitchen and see the size of the pot on the stove. If the pot was big, they could be sure of a meal at night. If the pot was small, they would have only lunch, no dinner. At such times, Annam would say to herself, "Had my father been alive, we would not have to suffer like this" and cry. After the cooking was over, her mother, she said, would keep five plates and divide the food equally and serve the children. But to the last child alone, she would give a little extra. The other children, without the knowledge of the mother, and unmindful of his crying, would snatch the extra food from the youngest boy's plate and eat it up. Such poverty exists throughout the world. Is it not our duty to alleviate the sufferings of these poor people?

"How far the little candle throws its beams, so shines a good deed in this naughty world."

15

Mother Teresa

"Giving opens the door for receiving". When a person gives freely and wholeheartedly he receives god's blessings. God pays back with full interest and dividends. This is a divine law. It pays higher interest than any bank. Great souls have always taught that among all the forms of giving, imparting the Spiritual teachings is the highest. Life is like a bank account. We get what we put.

When we do good, God is with us. He gives us the strength to bear whatever hardships we may come across in our endeavours. Hence, we can start doing good with complete faith in God. Faith moves mountains.

Take for example, Mother Teresa. When she first came to India, she had just forty rupees with her. "What can you do with only forty rupees", asked her friends. She replied confidently, "I have just forty rupees. But I have mountains of faith." When she approached people for donations in the dirty streets of Calcutta to build an ashram for the poor, it was difficult even to collect Rs. 25/- There were some wealthy men who were very generous, but there were others who railed against the Mother. But even to them, the Mother was sweet and smiling.

Today, the Institutions of Charity founded by Mother Teresa, are spread over 130 countries. Their annual income is Rupees Sixteen crores. Whether it was a leprosy centre in Canada, or a feeding centre in Kenya, the respective governments allotted land and funds. Whenever the Mother bought things for her 'homes', shopkeepers vied with one another in supplying the goods free. The words of the Mother who cared for leprosy patients and AIDS patients alike, carried much weight and were highly respected in foreign countries. In short, with just forty rupees and tons of confidence as her capital, Mother Teresa moved mountains with the simple tool of her infinite love. When she died, her only belongings were a bucket and two sarees. The whole world mourned her passing away. Around the same time, the world mourned the death of Princess Diana, who had devoted much of her time for the betterment of the underprivileged. Great leaders and millionaires sometimes leave the world unsung and unwept for. To those who indulged in female infanticide, Mother Teresa had said, "Don't kill the girl child, Jesus lives in every child. So give these children to me."

Life is very short. Time and tide wait for none. As the good that we do returns to us, let us do as much good as we can, as quickly as we can. It is best to do good without expecting any rewards. Each one of us would like to become like Mother Teresa. But when someone seeks our help, many of us are unwilling to render that help. In reality, we should be thankful to those who come to us asking for help; because, indirectly they give us an opportunity to do some good.

To begin with, we can start doing little acts of kindness. The joy and mental satisfaction that we derive from doing these little acts will serve as motivation for us to do greater acts of good. We should remember that big things are only multiplications or intensified forms of little things. Hence, let us begin doing good today itself. The world will then become a better place to live in

"The more you spend your energy in serving others, the more divine energy will flow to you"
—*Swami Vivekanantha*

16

All men are good

There is a story to illustrate the fact that nobody is bad in this world. A lady and her daughter-in-law were always at loggerheads with one another. One day, the daughter-in-law went to a physician and asked for some poison that would kill her mother-in-law so gradually that none would suspect her of the murder. The doctor gave a cream which he said was poisoned; he instructed her to apply the cream on her mother-in-law's arms and legs. The daughter-in-law obeyed the doctor's instructions and massaged her mother-in-law's arms and legs daily. Overwhelmed by the loving care with which the daughter-in-law treated her, the lady stopped quarrelling with her daughter-in-law. Instead, she began to be affectionate towards her. The daughter-in-law regretted here decision to kill her mother-in-law. She went to the doctor and said, "I am very sorry for having plotted to kill my mother-in-law. Please give me an antidote for the poison. I don't want her to die." The doctor laughed and said, "I anticipated this change of heart in you. There is no poison in the cream I gave you. You can return home peacefully." The daughter-in-law was very happy. She continued to be good to her mother-in-law who is turn loved her as if she were her own daughter. If we want our detractors to become our friends, we should be doubly good to them. Love will always be recompensed with love only. As there is a 'spark of divinity' in each one of us, all are worth of love and affection. Once we realize this 'natural' truth, there will be no room for squabbles and misunderstandings in this world.

Even murderers commit crimes only on an impulse. Later they regret their haste. However bad a person is, he will certainly have a few good qualities. If we appreciate those good qualities sincerely, they will become good in their earnestness to please us. On the other hand, if we keep on harping on their vices, they will never try to change. Instead, they will start hating us.

That even convicts can be reformed, has been proved by the prisoners in the Sabarmathi Jail Ahmedabad in Gujarat State. These prisoners get up at 4 a.m. and finish off all their work. They then prepare bread, biscuits, snacks etc., and send them out for sale. People queue up to buy these products. The prisoners also make footwear, bed spreads, handbags, and so on and sell them. The sale of these products had exceeded 3.5 crores. One of the prisoners, Ramji Patel had been a mechanic. Hence he produced a machine which could prepare 8000 chappathis in four hours.

If we avenge a wrong done to us, what is the difference between us and the wrong doer? There is nothing more despicable than returning evil for evil. If we do thus, it is the wrongdoer who will be considered the victor. We become his slaves. On the other hand, if we do good to the wrongdoer, he will regret his vile deed, be ashamed of his wickedness and become good. It is not enough if we are good. One good man can convert ten bad men into good men. These ten men can convert a hundred bad men. This is the way to change the world.

Hard things can be dissolved by soft things. Water is soft. But it is capable of dissolving any kind of dirt. It can penetrate even hard rocks. It then solidifies into ice and causes the rock to break. Love is a soft weapon. Love alone can enter even the hardest hearts.

Animals that are governed by their senses are so affectionate to those with whom they are familiar. Just a pat and some food is sufficient to make pets as loving as our own children. Scientists have now discovered that even plants react to loving words.

Many parents indulge in fault-finding and scolding their children. Such children are likely to suffer from mental disorders later in life. On the other hand, children who grow up in a healthy atmosphere turn out to be good citizens.

Taking revenge on an offender results in weakening us, because we lose our moral strength. Try to use then force of love. Let us join together and conquer the world with the power of love. I shall prove to you how strong love is, and how it can transform the very course of one's life, by narrating an incident from my own life.

The highest form of love is spiritual love. This kind of love is loving a person because we see God in him. This kind of love does not expect anything from anybody and does not find fault with anybody. It is love for the sake of love. This divine love radiates throughout the universe where every thing is in harmony.

"Great minds discuss ideas
Mediocre minds discuss events
Small minds discuss people."

17

Humility

Emperor Ashoka was walking along with his minister, outside the palace. A Buddhist monk came towards them from the opposite direction. On seeing the monk, the emperor immediately prostrated himself before the monk and sought his blessings.

After the monk had passed by, the minister expressed his feelings. "My Lord, you are such a great emperor. Why should you seek the blessings of a poor monk?"

The emperor did not reply. He just smiled.

The next day, the emperor summoned the minister and said, "Please go into the city and bring me a goat's head, a tiger's head and a man's head".

Puzzled by this strange command, the minister procured the items the king had asked for with great difficulty and presented them before the emperor.

The emperor now said, "Take these items into the market and see what value you can get for them".

With much distaste, the minister proceeded to execute the second strange command.

Once in the market, the goat's head was immediately purchased. The tiger's head took longer to sell. But not a single person wanted the human head. They shuddered with revulsion at the sight and walked away, turning their faces.

The minister went back to the palace and reported on the status to the emperor.

The emperor said, "Once life leaves our body, there is no value for it, be it the body of a king or a beggar. We should remember that and understand the greatness inherent in saints who have forsaken the worldly life for enlightenment. We should be very humble and acknowledge greatness in others".

From this story, we learn that we need to live without ego. Ego or self-importance is a man's greatest enemy.

18

Get the right perspective

It was a busy day in the market. A variety of wares were being sold and the market was bustling with activity.

A man was looking for a good horse to buy. He frequently had to travel across kingdoms for his business, and he was looking for a sturdy, well-bred horse that could move swiftly and untiringly across long distances.

He went to the section of the market where horses and other animals were being bartered or sold. He approached first one horse seller and then another, but was not satisfied. The third horse seller was a wizened old man who was surveying the scene with shrewd eyes. He had only one horse tied by his side, but it appeared to be a magnificent specimen of prime horseflesh.

The man approached the old horse seller and asked him for the price of the horse. The horse seller quoted a price that was exorbitantly high. The man was shocked.

"Even a horse made of gold and diamonds would not cost so much", he said.

"Ah, but my horse is very clever", the man explained. "When the rider falls down, the horse will find the way and carry him to the nearest hospital".

The man was impressed. He decided to buy the horse in spite of the high rate the seller demanded.

A month went by. It was market day again. The old horse seller was standing in his usual place when a man came rushing to him.

"You cheated me," the man shouted angrily. "Last month, you sold me a horse that you said was clever enough to take the rider to the hospital, in case of an accident".

"Did the horse do nothing when you had an accident?", the old man asked, thoughtfully.

"No, it did carry me away from the scene of the accident", the man replied furiously, "but to a vetinary hospital".

The old man smiled. "That shows that I did not cheat you. It did carry you to a hospital", he replied.

"Of what use is it to a human being to be taken to a vetinary hospital?", the man demanded.

"Ah, but the human being should have thought about that before he bought the horse. It is an animal. The only hospital it has ever been to is a vetinary hospital. How could you even expect that a horse would take you to a hospital for human beings", the man replied.

How often have we encountered such circumstances in our life? How many times have we felt frustrated and disappointed when others did not live up to our expectations? What we need to understand from this story is that every person behaves the way he does, either because of his circumstances or because of his ability.

If a wise man expects a foolish man to take the right decisions, he is bound to be disappointed. If a rich man expects his servant to think as he does, he will end up frustrated.

If we tone down our expectations and look at things from the perspective of the other person, we can avoid much disappointment and frustration in our life.

19

Boy and the bird

A boy had arrested a small bird within his hands. He asked Vivekananda if the bird in his hands was dead or alive. Vivekananda thought for a moment and answered thus—If I say that the bird is dead, you will leave it to fly and if I say that it is alive, you will crush the bird to death. So the fate of the bird is entirely in your hands!

Similarly our life is also entirely in our hands.

"Life is not attainment but a state of mind".

20

Buddha

One day a man came to Buddha and abused him with unpleasant words. Buddha sat calmly till the man was exhausted and stopped scolding.

Now Buddha asked the man gently and lovingly, "If someone brings you a gift and you do not want to accept, to whom the gift belongs?".

The man replied "This is really a foolish question. Surely if the gift is not accepted it remains with the giver".

Now Buddha replied softly "My friend I do not accept the words that you gave me!"

21

Loving words prevented suicide

In our town, a boy lost his father. Some years earlier, he had lost his mother. His sisters were married and were living in other towns. After the funeral rites were over, all the relatives left the place feeling that their duties were over. This boy was all alone in the house. He was orphaned and lonely. His eyes were swollen with crying. Unable to come to terms with the reality, he just sat there, staring at the sky.

I felt very sad for the boy. I told him, "Don't cry. Console yourself. Don't think that your are an orphan. My husband and myself are always with you. Whatever help you want, don't hesitate to ask us. We are ready to help you anytime". Having these words, his face brightened a little and he nodded his head.

However, not once did he approach us for any favour. Whenever I met him, I enquired about his health and gave him some sound advice. In course of time he married. Now he is the proud father of a sweet child. One day he came to me, took my hands in his and said gratefully. "When my father died, my life seemed shattered, If only you had not comforted me then, I would even have committed suicide. All that I am today, I owe to your fully."

Do you now understand the power of love? As a matter of fact, I had not done anything for that boy. He did not need any material help. All that he needed was a little love and consolation. A few loving words saved the boy from committing suicide. Why do words of love have such power? Because they come from the depths of our hearts. God dwells in our hearts, and love is the essence of God. In fact, Love is God. The expression of love is the greatest developer of the soul.

We are divine

Love that is greater than this very universe, dwells in all our hearts, There is no limit to love. Those of you, who have never been to an orphanage, please visit one. Take some eats, old clothes and things which you no longer require. See the joy lighting up the faces of the children there. Reflect on this experience when you go to bed. The happiness and satisfaction that you will feel, have to be experienced to be believed.

"Happiness is never perfect until shared
Do what you can, with what you have, right where you are."
—*Roosevelt*

Love dwells even in evil minds

Love dwells even in evil minds, because God lives in them also. The spark of divinity is in every being, regardless of race, colour or creed. It may not always be seen on the surface. It is our duty to awaken the latent divinity within us.

It is because we fail to recognize this, that there is unrest at home and outside. The source of all actions is the individual's heart. So let us have faith in the Divine spark which dwells in every heart, waiting to be awakened and developed.

Different rungs of the ladder

We are all on different rungs of the ladder of self-development. Some of us, through right reactions of life-experience, have become more spiritually advanced than others. But we must never forget that the opportunity exists for even the lowest to climb this ladder. Let us help him to do so. We must not make the mistake of considering one person more favoured by God because of his greater enlightenment. The higher we climb, the greater is our responsibility to help those who are less fortunate.

Impress others

We cannot compel anybody to think just as we do. But we can, through our fellowship and understanding, move the heart and soul of another person and cause him or her to realize that we possess something extra, which they may be inspired to seek within themselves. Thus we can change even the wicked people who come in contact with us, by our childlike simplicity.

Tolerance

Let us exercise great tolerance towards others. If we return good for evil and not show any resentment at their misdeeds, it will be a greater punishment to them than any attempt at retaliation. We must learn to probe the recesses of our soul. Once we have found the core of our being, the whole course of our life will change. The people whom we shrank from earlier will now appear dear to us, because our souls will be attuned to theirs. This will result in a permanent bond of love.

> *"Let me a little kinder*
> *Let me a little blinder*
> *To the faults of those around."*

22

Duty

A saint (who had acquired great mental power through meditation) was once returning after taking a bath, when a bird defiled him. The saint looked up angrily at the bird. Immediately, it was burnt to death. Such was the power of the saint's penance. Sometime later, the saint went to a house and begged for alms. The lady of the house saw him. But she had to take care of her husband and her aged parents-in-law. Only after their needs had been attended to, she came out with some food for the saint. The latter glared at her, angry at the delay. But the lady said calmly, "Do you think you can burn me also, as you burnt the bird?" The saint was astonished. How did this lady learn of the burning of the bird? It was because she had performed her duties to the best, that she had acquired powers greater than those possessed by the saint.

It is not the wrongdoers alone, who are guilty. Those who fail to do their duties, are also guilty. All religions advocate the performance of one's duties. Man is a social animal. We need and enjoy the services of several people. In our day-to-day life, we benefit directly or indirectly, from the services of the carpenter, the merchant, the plumber, the builder, the postman, the electrician and so many others. Hence, it is our duty to serve the society in some way or the other.

An uneducated old lady used to seek my help to write letters to her son who lived in another town. I too obliged her willingly. All those letters were supplications for financial assistance. The money was needed for medical expenses and for her daughter's confinement. Ironically however, not one of these letters received any response from her son. Undeterred, the mother continued to write letters. Having lost my patience, I once asked her, "You have written so many letters. But your son has neither replied nor sent any money. Why do you waste your money and energy thus?" The old lady replied, "I'm writing these letters in the hope that one day he may change his mind and send me some money." I was surprised at the lady's faith. At the same time, the son's indifference made me hate him. In the meantime, the old lady died. Till the end, she never received any help from her son. I felt that instead of begetting such a child, she could have remained childless. Every man should regard his parents (who had made several sacrifices to bring him up) as a living God and serve them till their death.

If he fails to do this, he cannot be said to have done his duty to an unseen God, no matter how religious he is. When their children take loving care of them, parents are overjoyed and they bless the children wholeheartedly. We can see God in their happiness.

Statistics show that the number of aged people being admitted into old-age homes is increasing.

"As a white candle in a holy place, so is the beauty of an aged face."

This universe knows no rest. Nature sees to it that we do not remain idle even for moment. With the exception of our sleeping hours, our minds are always active even if our bodies are at rest. Hence, to remain idle is unnatural. An idle mind is the devil's workshop.

People believe that only saints can reach God. This is not true. Those who do their duties sincerely and offer them to God, are eligible to reach God. If all of us were to renounce the world and become saints, how will the world be maintained? How will future generations evolve? Hence, we should carry out our duties without deceiving others. That is real dedication.

Here is a short story about the greatness of 'duty'. In a certain village there was no rain for twelve years. But there was a farmer who continued to plough his field systematically. Surprised, the Rain God appeared before him and asked, "There has been no rain here for the past twelve years. Why do you waste your energy ploughing?" The farmer replied, "Ploughing is my occupation. If I don't practise it, I will forget it. That is why I continue to practise it." The Rain God felt ashamed at His failure to His duty, and sent down rain. The man who does not do his duty, is wasting his potential.

23

Greed

We have come across people who have risen from penury to affluence. The success of those who become rich through unfair means, will have only a false glitter. It is transitory and may make today's millionaire tomorrow's pauper. Money that comes through hard work and fair means alone, will be lasting. The world may scoff at such people (who believe in hard work) dubbing them incompetent. But that does not matter.

That greed can prompt a man to do anything, can be illustrated by a story. Four friends, A,B,C,D struck upon a buried treasure. There was serious disagreement on the issue of sharing the treasure. As a result, they fought with one another; A was killed. The other three were by now hungry. So, B was sent to fetch some food. When he returned, he found C dead. He asked D how C died. "Thus", said D and clubbed B to death with a huge stone. D exulted at the fact that he was now the sole owner of the treasure. He opened the food packet eagerly and ate the food. In a short while, he also died. B had plotted to kill both C and D with poisoned food, so that he could enjoy the treasure himself. Thus, greed brought about the death of four men who had been close friends.

24

The son who bit his mother's ear

A mother had trained her young son to steal. After he grew up, he became a professional robber. But one day he was caught and produced in the court. He requested the judge to allow him to see his mother just once, before he was sent to prison. His request was granted. When his mother came, he approached her and bit off one of her ears. All those who were present were shocked and asked him why he did such a thing. He replied, "If my mother had brought me up properly and taught me good things, I would never have been here today."

We can see that a mother is responsible for tainting society itself. Every one of our actions, from morning till night, should be dedicated to God. Religion is not something external. We have to 'live' it. It should govern all our deeds.

Every thought and act of ours, has its repercussions in the universe and in nature. It has been said that, if a butterfly flitters its wings in Tokyo, a leaf may tremble in Manila. Our very breath has an impact on the universe. Mind creates; mind also destroys.

Some people say, "We are very good;" but their actions betray them. Those who adulterate foodstuffs do not worry about the consequences of their deeds on the consumers. They think that patriotism involves only the hoisting of the national flag. True patriotism lies in not deceiving our own countrymen. Some people believe that they can earn money through unfair means, but if they offer a certain percentage of their earning to God, it will balance the wrong that they have committed. Can God be bribed? Such a misunderstanding exists, because people have understood the value of money; but they have not understood the value of truthfulness. Let us tear the veil of ignorance and recognize our true nature, and know that we are children of Light and not of darkness.

It is said of Mohammed that his uncle tried to dissuade him from his religious ardor, as it was making him unpopular among people. He offered him a large sum of money if he would keep quiet about his faith. This was Mohammed's answer. "If you give me the sun in one hand and the moon in other, I should not give up." Saints would not exchange their treasure for the richest material possession. Nothing could tempt them.

25

Mother's kindness

A young man fell in love with a beautiful but cruel girl. This girl knew that the man loved his mother dearly. So she said to him "Cut out your mother's heart and bring it to me as a token of your love towards me".

Blinded by passion, the man killed his mother as she slept. He cut out her heart and stole out to his lover's house in that dark night.

In the darkness, he stumbled on a stone and fell down. The mother's heart dropped out of his hands.

Now he heard his mother say "My dear son, are you hurt?"

26

The benefits of meditation

Practising meditation (through concentration) without asking God for any favours, can yield many benefits. Let us see what they are:

1. God is the embodiment of all good qualities. When we meditate, our minds absorb the good qualities of God unconsciously. These qualities serve to light up our soul.
2. In today's stressful world, the word most often used and heard, is 'tension'. If a man suffers from tension, he takes it out on his poor wife. The wife, on her part, takes it out on the innocent children. We have seen several families ruined in this manner. But those who practise mediation, will never have any tension. They will be able to approach any problem patiently and sensibly.
3. When people are beset with difficulties and are worried, they resort to drinking. This will offer only temporary relief, and is not a permanent solution. Mediation can be permanent solution. Drinking can lead to financial loss, ill health, anxiety to others in the family, humiliation, and sometimes even death.

4. In every man's life there are bound to be crises. It is in such situations, that cowards commit suicide. But when we meditate,

    a) Our thoughts become purer, because of concentration.
    b) When our thinking is clear, we are able to discriminate between right and wrong.
    c) We become clear-sighted.
    d) Hence we become confident of ourselves.
    e) We are able to carry out duties properly. "Right thinking leads to right doing."

5. Some people suffer from depression due to over-anxiety. Because of this, their mind is affected and they behave abnormally. Then they consult psychiatrists. The medicines prescribed by them give the patients an artificial peace of mind and therefore lead to harmful side-effects. But when we practise meditation, our mind, muscles and nerves are all relaxed. As we become one with God, we forget our sorrows, and attain peace and happiness. Thus we can spread joy, love and peace to all those around us.

6. It has been established through research that meditation helps to cure many diseases that affect the body. When we sit in one place and meditate, our breathing is regulated. This is not only beneficial to the heart, but also for stabilizing the blood pressure. As we meditate intensely, our breathing becomes deeper. Our oxygen intake increases and the carbondioxide exhalation also increases proportionately. Normally we breathe in half a volume of oxygen and breathe out half a volume of carbondioxide. This amount is inadequate and therefore

does not reach our fingers and toes. Some of the cells in the lungs too, do not receive sufficient oxygen. Because of this some parts of our body do not function properly and the mind is disturbed. Our lungs are the heaviest part of our body. Hence we can see how important it is for us to receive adequate supply of oxygen.

7. I find many students lacking in self confidence. We will never meet with failure if we can do our work with perfect attention and concentration. If an ordinary person takes one hour to do a work, a man of good concentration (attained through meditation) will accomplish it in half an hour better efficiency than the former. We can become a mighty person. Concentration is the masterkey to open the gates of victory.

8. It is on the surface of the sea that we come across waves and other disturbances. But deeper down, the sea is very calm and undisturbed. When we meditate we journey to the depths of our mind where peace dwells. At such moments, the cosmic energy which pervades the world but is invisible enters our being. We call this spiritual strength. It was by the use of this spiritual strength, that great men like Gandhi achieved many unique victories. In other words, when through meditation our full mental energy unites with divine energy, we are able to achieve great things. Prayer serves to link our efforts with God's power. We can save up this energy just like a battery being recharged. We can use it whenever necessary. Only those who see the Invisible can do the impossible. We are surrounded by an ocean of cosmic energy. We can energise our body through meditation. In the previous chapters we learnt about the benefits of going to temples and worshipping God.

All religions advocate fasting. Fasting serves to protect our physical and mental health. Through fasting, we can rid ourselves of harmful toxins that could lead to diseases. All the important organs like the heart, kidneys, intestines and liver, are invigorated. Our body is made up of the five elements of water, land, air, fire and sky. These very five elements serves medicines also. When we fast, the intestines and the stomach become empty. Then the sky serves as medicine. Moreover, when we fast, we realize what hunger is and we are able to sympathise with the poor who are hungry. Thus our kindness and generosity are increased. We learn humility, discipline and self control. That is why our forefathers practiced fasting and enjoyed its benefits. It will be good if we too can practise fasting, according to our capacity.

By means of meditation we acquire the mental maturity to show love and affection towards all men equally. We have been created only to love, help one another, and thus be happy. It is through meditation that we can transcend all barriers of caste, creed, language, nationality, race, and realize that we are all children of one God. In such a state, only the language of love is legal tender.

Some people think of God only when they are weighed down with sorrow. This is not the right approach. A mango tree will not yield mangoes through magic. Misfortunes do not announce their arrival. They come unexpectedly. Hence, the meditation that we have been practicing everyday, has the power to reduce or even negate the sorrow that may befall us. Moreover, meditation gives us the strength to withstand whatever sorrow that may befall us, just as a rock withstands the constant buffeting of the waves.

We have often come across people, who, at crucial moments in their lives are at a loss to decide on the course of action to be taken. Those who practise meditation regularly, will never face a situation like this. They will be able to think clearly and take the right decision; one that will lead to long-term benefits. An inner voice will guide them. Moreover, meditation gives enlightenment. And solutions to doubts and problems will automatically dawn on us.

Meditation can be described as the ability to use mental power to achieve success. There no limit to mental strength. For example, let us assume that a man who is accustomed to waking up at six every morning, has to go out of station. He plans to wake up at four a.m. Before going to bed, he just has to meditate and tell himself that he has to wake up at four. Without the use of an alarm clock, he can wake up at four. Undoubtedly, the greatest power on earth is the power of the mind. The man who can control his mind, can control the entire world. Concentration is the masterkey to open the gates of victory. Light waves, like sound waves, cannot travel very far. But thought waves can travel from one end of the world to the other. Telepathy, hypnotism, mesmerism and distant healing all function with the help of mental power. Thought has tremendous power indeed! It is only through meditation that we can increase the power of our mind. By means of meditation, we can progress in life; we can achieve anything.

Arjuna had wonderful concentration. He learnt the science of archery from Dronacharya. A dead bird was tied to a post in such a way that its reflection was cast in a basin of water right below on the ground. Arjuna aimed successfully in hitting at the right eye of the actual bird tied to the post above, by seeing the reflection of the bird in the basin of water. Napoleon also had remarkable power of concentration. It is said that he had full control over his thoughts.

We can derive several benefits from the practice of meditation. But people believe that through meditation we can ask God for material benefits. And when we don't get them, we give up meditation, saying that it is useless. This is wrong.

Our soul is a gift from God. Though the power of our soul is unlimited, it will remain unavoidable and unrecognizable until we reach sufficient spiritual development (through meditation) to utilize it. Let us free our mind of false concepts and become a real force of goodness. Unfortunately evil exists because man has allowed his soul to slumber. He finds a crooked way (short-cut) to attain everything without any effort on his part

We should all practise meditation and obtain its benefits. I am writing this book because I want everyone to receive God's blessings and live happily.

An important factor (which we should remember about meditation) is that those who do not perform their duties well and those who hurt others, will not derive any benefits from meditation. God will not accept it, because God is the embodiment of love, So, only if our hearts are full of love, can we feel the presence of God. Those who hurt others can never reach God, no matter how many pilgrim centres they visit.

I have a request for my dear readers. Do not stop meditating, saying that it has not given you any benefit. Meditation is a continual process. For example, a huge oak tree is hidden in an acorn. We should sow the seed of devotion, water it with the water of duty and good deeds, manure it with meditation, weed out evil thoughts and deeds, and construct a fence that will keep out bad qualities. Only then can we reach sublime heights, A bright future awaits us there. Remember, Rome was not built in a day. In your failure lies the secret of your success. Be bold. Plod on. Push on. March courageously. It is all a question of time.

Students and youth in general, should recognize their hidden power and come forward to serve our motherland.

The world needs young and strong hands like yours. May you be the light of the world.

When should we meditate?

It is difficult to find leisure in this world of hurry and stress. Hence, whenever we find time we can meditate. However, it is best to meditate early in the morning. After some good rest also, our body and mind will be fresh enough to meditate. We can meditate at sunset and before going to bed. Working women hardly find time to meditate as they have their household duties as well. When they perform their duties well, that itself is equal to meditation. Nevertheless, they can meditate even during a bus journey or a short break at the office.

How long should we meditate?

The longer we meditate, the better it is for us. But it will be good if we can meditate for half an hour in the morning, and half an hour in the evening. We can cut down the time that we watch the TV. Just as we allot time for physical exercise or attending computer classes, we can also find time for meditation. No pain, no gain. Only if we work hard, we can succeed. Only by melting gold, can we make beautiful ornaments.

When should we start meditation?

Children should be taught about God and worship at an early age. We should explain this to them in simple words or through the medium of stories. By means of puranic stories, we can impress upon their minds the fact that good will triumph and evil will be defeated. History tells us that Swami Vivekananda and Chatrapathi Shivaji were nurtured with such stories by their respective mothers. Children are like soft clay. We can mould them as we wish. Parents should not think that their duty towards their children is only to feed, clothe and educate them. From an early age parents should instill in their children courage and self confidence. Only then will the children learn to face failures and disappointments and not resort to suicide.

It is the mother who has a large share in bringing up the child. It is from the mother that a child learns good habits and qualities. A good mother is an asset to the nation because she begets good children. The father is the second teacher to the child. The class teacher is the third. All the three teachers are only guides. They can guide us like a stationary signpost. Using their guidance, we have to take the effort and travel along the right path. God will lead and enlighten us. Top rankers in any exam will always say that they were inspired and encouraged by their parents and teachers.

Elders have many duties and responsibilities. Children are free birds. Hence they will have a lot of time. Moral science should be made a compulsory subject in schools. That alone can provide us with solutions to all our problems. We need education that will make man 'human'. That alone is complete education. Childhood lost is livelihood lost. Character should be strengthened by discipline.

Thanksgiving

We should teach children right from childhood, to offer thanks to God. We should also teach them to thank people for favours received. Thanksgiving is a very good trait in men. I remember a song which we were taught when we were in 1ˢᵗ Standard.

> *"Thank you God for the world so sweet,*
> *Thank you God for the food we eat,*
> *Thank you God for the birds that sing,*
> *Thank you God for everything."*

I am extremely grateful now to the teacher who taught me to offer thanks to God for everything.

Vessel with a hole

Here is a short story. Before leaving for the market, a mother asked her daughter to fill all the vessels with water. The daughter did as she was told. But when the mother returned, she was shocked to find all the vessels empty. This was because all the vessels had a hole each. A man without character, is like a vessel with a hole. Having everything, he has nothing. Nature does not deviate from the path of righteousness. Hence, we should also teach our children sound values and the importance of good conduct.

27

The Prince and the Sage

A wise king ruled a prosperous kingdom. He was renowned for his patience and far-sightedness. To groom the crown-prince for his future role, the king decided to send him to the ashram of a famous sage, who was known far and wide for his ascetic life style and concentration and meditation techniques.

The prince arrived at the sage's ashram, full of hopes and dreams of quickly mastering the most complicated of meditation techniques and demonstrating his skills to the awe-struck subjects of his kingdom.

The prince was warmly received at the ashram. He was given the saffron robes that were the attire of the disciples at the ashram. He took part in a simple meal of fresh fruits and simple cereals. He then waited eagerly for his training to begin.

On the first day, he was given the task of cleaning the entire ashram. He was taken aback at being given such a menial task, but went ahead and did the job to the best of his ability. He expected that his meditation classes would start the next morning and went to sleep in a mood of eager anticipation.

However, the next morning, he was again asked to repeat the same task of cleaning the ashram—he was annoyed this time. He, a crown prince, doing such menial tasks! Wouldn't his subject laugh and jeer if they could see him now! Was this what he came to the ashram for? he fumed, as he went about the cleaning tasks with gritted teeth. That night, his mood was not so pleasant and he slept fitfully.

On the third day, he went with an arrogant attitude, fully expecting to start his meditation training. To his extreme fury, he was again asked to repeat the same task. This time, his anger knew no bounds. As he was cleaning the kitchen area, he glanced around. At a distance, he saw the sage in deep meditation. Without thought, he grabbed a kitchen knife and ran towards the sage, intending to stab him for the insults heaped on him over the last three days.

As he neared the sage, the sage broke out of his deep meditation and opened his eyes and regarded him out of calm and wise eyes.

"What are you doing?, he asked in a gentle voice.

The young prince was stunned. "How did you know that I was coming to harm you?" he asked, the knife falling out of his hand to the ground.

"My son, don't you know that meditation has a multitude of benefits. It helps to develop intuition and improves one's ability to react to danger. It increases our awareness of external happenings and I can even feel the air around me stir when someone approaches me. Now, tell me the reason for this rage?"

The prince fell at the sage's feet and begged forgiveness for his thoughtless intent. From that moment, he changed from an arrogant young man to a humble person with a deeper understanding of the power of meditation. He spent many months at the sage's ashram and acquired the meditation skills. Eventually, he returned to his kingdom, a wiser and more balanced man, whom the people were proud to receive as their leader.

Thus we learn from this story that regular practice of meditation will help to improve peace of mind and happiness, help us to keep things in perspective and changes our attitude towards life. It will help us to increase awareness to external surroundings and to react quickly and in the right manner to stressful situations.

28

The power of the soul

We learnt that the power of the soul is unlimited. This can be understood by the fact that, thousands of years ago, without the aid of sophisticated scientific instruments, Indians were able to discover scientific truths which modern scientists have now discovered. Let us see what they are,

Indians knew the position of the various planets and how they move in space due to the power of gravity.

They knew that water contained one part oxygen and two parts of other gases; also that the soil on the surface of the moon was black.

That water from the ocean evaporates into a cloud and later comes down as rain, was mentioned by Andal in her devotional songs composed in the 9th century.

Another interesting fact is that our ancestors knew that light from the sun takes eight minutes to reach the earth. Hence, they performed 'Surya Namaskaram' (Salutation to the Sun God) eight minutes before sunrise and sunset respectively.

How to realise the power of the soul

We know about the conscious mind, and about the sub-conscious mind very well. But when we meditate, our mind reaches the super-conscious state.

Problems can be solved

Our conscious mind is problem-oriented. But the super-conscious, with its broader, more comprehensive view, is solution-oriented. The comprehensive view is justified objectively in Nature. Every natural problem has a corresponding solution. Native Americans claim that whenever a poisonous plant grows, an antidote will be growing nearby. If we place matters with complete trust in God's hands, things will always work out best, provided we follow the path of righteousness. We must conquer all our baser propensities.

A scientific truth

If an electrical connection is given to a refrigerator, it starts cooling. If the same connection is given to an iron box, it begins to get hot. If a bulb is switched on, we get light. If a tape recorder is switched on, we get sound. But all these are dependent for their functioning on electricity. In the same manner, although we may perform various tasks, that which directs those tasks, is our soul or spirit. Our body functions are controlled by our brain. But we should not forget that the brain itself is controlled by our soul. The more we cultivate our moral strength, the more we can discover that part of our being which is infinite. Unfortunately man has permitted his soul to slumber.

Don't worry

Every problem will have a solution. Difficulties are bound to arise, but they are not permanent. Whenever we meet with difficulties, we must remember that they born of finite conditions and are bound to disappear. Our problems are self-made, by our opposing the laws of the universe. The laws of the universe operate impersonally and automatically. The rain falls on the just and unjust alike. Man is constantly punishing himself by willful disobedience of these laws. So the fundamental teaching of the Bhagavat Gitas ia "Don't worry". This is because, the solution is always with us, but we are looking all around for it.

Let us plumb the depths of the mind

Let us plumb into the depths of our mind. Let us remove the stains of our mistakes and thus conquer sorrow. Peace is power. Flowers blossom quietly. The sun rises quietly. We must know the root cause of all our sorrows. And unless we strike at the roots of our sorrows, we will not be able to solve our problems and achieve happiness.

It has been proved scientifically, that only if there is a vacancy, something can fill it. Only if our mind is totally empty, divine thoughts will fill it. Some people sit down to meditate, but begin to think about their problems. This is of no use. We should not allow our minds to be employed with problems. Jesus said, "Empty thyself and I shall fill thee."

Meditation

Meditation is not a mechanical repetition of verses. Our mind should dissolve itself into the divine grace of God. That is true meditation. The world is full of sorrows. Any moment, we may be overcome by misfortune. Therefore, dear friends, meditate! meditate! meditate. Never waste your precious time. This does not mean that you should not watch the TV or see films. Recreation is necessary. But is should be within limits. You should not become addicted to the TV. God is ever seeking the co-operation of man and man must ever seek the co-operation of God.

Om, Alla, Amen, Amma—By constantly repeating these words we can improve our mental stamina as well as physical stamina. Saints attained salvation by doing so. The purpose of life is to manifest our divinity and saints are beacon lights who showed us the path. Let us move towards purity, towards gentleness, towards calmness and finally towards God.

God is present in all of us. Through proper self control we should invoke our hidden potentiality which is the source of success and consolation. There is no need to wait for external help. We must derive strength from our inner core.

Even if one door seems to be closed, God never fails to open another. Instead of waiting for opportunities it is wise to create opportunities.

29

Blessing in disguise

A man was shipwrecked and he found himself in an uninhabited island. He somehow managed to build a hut out of branches and leaves.

Everyday he would go out to the seashore and wave his hands in the hope that some passing steamer would see him and come to his rescue. Everyday evening he would return to his hut.

One evening as he returned he found that the hut had caught fire. He started cursing God with all the harsh words from the dictionary!

However he found a small steamer waiting for him at the seashore the next morning. The captain of the steamer explained that the fire from the island made him feel that there might be someone there who needed help.

Now the man on the island thanked God!

30

Faith

One thing that is abundantly found in a healthy personality is faith in oneself—faith in our Divinity. He has faith in himself and faith in others. Faith gives us hope and courage to pursue whatever one takes up. Faith, unquestionable faith, is the secret of success in any field. Behind every action stands faith, and greater an action, greater is the faith behind it.

Let us reflect on the following anecdote: A village was reeling under a severe drought. People were struggling to survive. One morning they were all surprised to see a sage sitting in front of the old temple. They all went to him and begged to pray to Varuna, the God of rain.

The sage nodded his head in agreement and said, "Fine. I will pray on one condition—that you should have implicit faith. No one should have any doubt". All the villagers shouted in one voice. "We have full faith in you". The sage said, "I will pray and all of you must assemble in front of this temple to welcome the Rain God tomorrow morning". They all agreed and dispersed.

Next morning, the entire village assembled in front of the temple. The sage looked at them and said, pointing to a child, "Well you want rain? None of you believe in it. None! None! except for this little child. "The villagers were shocked by his remarks. They looked at the child. The sage with a smile said, "Look at this child! Having total faith in me, he has brought an umbrella". The child had full faith that the sage will bring rain through his prayers. Such must be our faith.

Spirituality is hopeful and comforting. Hope for a future life, makes this life worthwhile; joyous, contented and happy. What we are now is the sum total of our past deeds. So what? The future is there for us. What we do now decides our future. So it is wise to strive hard on the little things in life as well as on the great challenges. We are the carvers of our own future. God's grace, His love is always blessing us in our efforts. It is well said that, 'Man is the maker of his own destiny.'

A great scientist was experimenting with a new technology and was repeatedly failing in his attempt. After making nearly hundred attempts, he finally succeeded in making the invention. Someone who had seen him struggling and succeeding asked him curiously, "Did you not feel discouraged by repeated failures? You failed so many times!" The scientist calmly replied "No. I now know ninety nine methods in which that invention could not have been made!"

Indeed people with healthy personality are always positive and hence they are stress-free.

> Those who win never quit.
> Those who quit never win.

If we are in a dark room, no amount of protestation will make it any brighter. We must light a match. No amount of grumbling and wailing helps us. Instead of finding fault we must find remedy.

Children should be taught that life is a battlefield and not a bed of roses. The world is not a bowl of cherries. We must make them understand that failures and difficulties are a part and parcel of our life. Victory and defeat are the two sides of a single coin.

Faith is a powerful force. Some people have faith only when things are going right, and lose faith when things go wrong. A person who has faith in God believes in the process of spiritual enfoldment, so that when he is going through a bitter experience, he always believes that the process is happening, instead of thinking that today's negative experience is outside the process.

We have faith in a person, a family, science, astronomy, astrology and so on. But faith in God is the most tenuous and delicate kind and the most rewarding of all faiths, because once it is sustained in unbroken continuity, the pure soul of the individual begins to shine forth.

So even in the midst of difficulties we can find quiet happiness if we have patience for the cosmic law to work out. That is growth.

The problem for us is, the longer we are on the path, the further the Goal seems to recede from us. Not that we move further from the goal, but we begin to realize how vast the goal is and how meager our best efforts are. So we have to stand up and be strong. There is salvation only for the brave. The sign of life is strength and growth. There is no other way out. We have to take a step higher and each step on the journey, with the constant aid of God, is a step toward greater and greater self-fulfillment ending in absolute Self-fulfillment.

31

Youth

Nowadays stress is a common problem. Stress is the reaction to a demanding situation such as fear, tension, anxiety, anger, emotional conflicts and so on. These situations may be of just a short period, but may affect a person for a long time, leaving deep impressions on the subconscious mind.

Meditation provides valuable guidelines to overcome stress and restlessness. There is a wrong notion among the youth that meditation is meant for old and retired people. But by sincere and serious practice of meditation such misnomers and false perceptions can surely be erased from the mind.

A youth, who has to prove his ability and rise up to the expectations of society, peers and others, undergoes a taxing time and it results in accumulation of stress. With many things to do, he lives a fast life and then there is no time to take stock of things. The modern youth may be thinking and working more than what his counterparts did earlier twenty years ago, but, then at what cost? psychological break-down and restlessness. At the same time when they are supposed to carry out their responsibilities, a little failure or a small obstacle here and there makes them feel weak and totally helpless. Some even think of running away from life itself.

These problems must be worked out with a positive attitude and high energy and a helping hand from God. Meditation goes to the root of the problem—setting right our world-view and resultant thinking. Once our thoughts change, there is visible change in quality of our actions and also our response to the results. Meditation helps us to change from within. Unlike psychological treatments it has no side effects.

Running away from problems and challenges of life does not solve them.

It only weakens the mind and makes it more incapable to face them in future. Drinks and drugs are not solutions. How does meditation solve this problem? When a person is mentally disturbed, we must understand that he is not inwardly strong. So it goes without saying that his inward mind must be strengthened. Meditation means turning our mind inward. A new inner process begins to take place. And little by little we find that we are turning inward, opening up the inner channels more and more each day, making a greater and greater contact with God, by turning within, drawing ourselves closer to the pole at the centre, the core of our Being.

Now there is no need to seek help from anyone. We are our own help. If we cannot help ourselves, there is none to help us. During meditation the mind is disciplined and becomes perfectly still like a lamp placed in a windless place. The calmer we are the better for us. Calmness is the mother of tremendous energy. Now we become confident. Our positive state of mind gains confidence. Negative people are always confused and worried about themselves. While we meditate, through silence and quieting of our mind, the spirit within us is intensified within us and it heals all the wounds that the mind may have.

Positive always overcome negative. Courage overcomes fear. Patience overcomes anger. Love overcomes hatred. This is the law of nature. Undoubtedly meditation bestows all these positive powers. We must remember that man contains within himself vast resources, inherent power lying untapped. Only meditation brings out our hidden power. So, mental weaknesses will vanish. The mind becomes stronger and stronger and there is no more stress.

If an ordinary man takes one hour to do a work, a man who meditates will accomplish in half an hour with better concentration and better efficiency than the former. Since the mind becomes calm, we can think clearly and think wisely. So whenever we want to take any important decision, we will be able to take the correct decision. Haste is always waste.

God is not only strength; but he strengthens us. So, He brings back what we lack and preserves what we already have. So whatever we do to improve ourselves remains with us. No effort goes vain. So whenever stressed, we should remember that God is the embodiment of strength, light, power, knowledge, wisdom, glory and joy.

So we can meditate thus-

Thou art embodiment of light, fill me with light.
Thou art embodiment of strength, fill me with strength.
Thou art embodiment of power and wisdom
Grant power and wisdom unto me.

—And so on. If this practice is done regularly, it will take away a good deal of stress and weakness of mind.

Let every youth try to renew his life by doing so. Thus he can achieve internal equilibrium. All the inner enemies in the battlefield like stress, fear, tension and sorrow are automatically slain. We also feel a spiritual current growing within. Our problems will gradually dissolve and our spiritual life will become a blessing to ourselves and others.

The posture is very important while we sit to meditate. We should always sit up straight with the spine erect. In such a position we cannot be worried, fretful or depressed. But if we slump the shoulders forward it is easy to become depressed and unhappy. So we have to sit dynamically, relaxed and yet poised. With the spine erect and the head balanced, the life force is quickened and intensified as energies flood freely through the nervous system Most of our vital organs are activated in this position. We can also save on doctor's bill through meditation. The Divine vibrations penetrate all the cells of our body and cure many diseases. The usage of computers and vehicles weakens the spine. By sitting up straight, the spine is strengthened.

Fairy Tale Concept

We must not be too hasty in longing for the fruits at once, when you take to meditation. A common man wants to get everything immediately, be it solving his worldly problems or getting to experience God. He is willing to undergo hardships to get a job. He works for hours together in the office. But he is not ready to spare even half an hour per day for meditation!

If we plant a tree we have to wait for it to grow and mature before we enjoy the shade. So it is with meditation. We have to work gently to develop a new life-style for the totality of our being—physically, emotionally, intellectually and spiritually. This we do a little at a time. Wisdom tells us that it cannot be done all at once. If we are impatient on the path, failure is in view. Instant spiritual enfoldment is a fairy tale concept. We must remember that Rome was not built in a day. No pain, No gain!

An ordinary man relies on his own strength. But a man, who meditates, unites his power with God's power and becomes stronger. We must know the basic law. We reap what we sow. Hence we alone are responsible for our sufferings and our happiness, our progress as well as our failures. This is a basic law. Therefore meditation is a must for all human beings. Meditation purifies the soul. Our sins are burnt. God assures that if a devotee sincerely leads a spiritual life relying on Him, He will not abandon him. Not only is the devotee protected, God stands by him under all circumstances.

What is needed is constant effort. A controlled mind is one's greatest friend and an uncontrolled mind is one's worst enemy. Daily meditation regulates our nervous system and the quality of our work improves. The calmness that we experience as a result of meditation is the natural state of our mind. We are not using our memory faculty. We are not using our reasoning faculty. But we are simply resting within ourselves. This is the most peaceful state of mind. Now we can have a clear perception of how we should behave in the external world. So let us move the forces of the world rightly, dynamically, intelligently, quickly and make something of our lives.

So a child should be taught how to pray and worship. If it is done so, he will derive great spiritual benefit in later life. Offering flowers in home—altar or temples, making them memorize divine songs and teaching them the simple meaning of holy scriptures will lay a strong foundation to a child's spiritual education. Sixty years later, the one-time child, would look back on the past with a sense of fulfillment. Thus we build the children into fine citizens.

32

Obstacles

A story is told about the famous Greek philosopher Socrates, who once asked his disciples, "What do you want to become in future?" One of them said that he wanted to become a lawyer, another wanted to become a politician, so on and so forth. But one conscientious student told that he wanted to become a man. Becoming a true man or woman has not been made a part of education. However man-making is not part of education unfortunately. That is why; various kinds of obstacles obstruct the path of a person who practices meditation. They do not make any solid progress.

The first obstacle is anger. It is a gate to hell. It is the greatest enemy of peace. A person when he is angry will talk anything he likes and do anything he likes. He commits murder. A hot word results in fighting and stabbing. That is why anger is called temporary madness! All vices and evil qualities take their origin in anger. When the anger assumes a grave form, it becomes difficult to control. Therefore we should nip it in the bud. Anger is a sign of mental weakness.

Sometimes anger is used to correct another person. It is used unselfishly as a force to check and improve him. Then it is called 'righteous anger'. Suppose a man molests a girl and tries to outrage her and a by-stander becomes angry towards this criminal, then it is called 'righteous indignation'. This is not bad. Only when the anger is the outcome of greed or selfish motives, it is bad.

But even when anger is used for a proper reason, one should be cool within and hot outside. It should pass off immediately like a wave in the sea. We should not curse even those who harm us. There is a story illustrating this factor.

There once lived a snake in a village. The snake used to bite everybody. Some died. The villagers were very much worried and complained about the snake to a sage. The sage advised the snake not to hurt anybody and also taught the snake a mantra. He asked the snake to chant the mantra all the time. The snake obeyed the sage. It became very pious, always chanting the mantra. From then onwards it did not bite anybody. The villagers were very happy. They were not frightened. So some people threw stones at the snake and the snake was almost torn to pieces. The sage who happened to see the snake was shocked. He asked the snake what happened and the snake explained everything. The sage replied, "Oh! Foolish snake! I asked you not to bite, but I did not tell you that you should not threaten them or frighten them!" Likewise, we should not harm anybody, but we can threaten them if they harm us.

Doctors say that all diseases take their origin in anger. Rheumatism, heart diseases and nervous diseases are due to anger. The whole nervous system is completely shattered by one fit of anger. Blood pressure rises. So, one should control anger completely to the very root.

Doubt:

Some people begin to doubt whether God exists or not, whether they will succeed in the process of meditation or not and so on. Lack of faith is a dangerous thing. Doubt is our great enemy. It causes restlessness of mind. When doubts try to overpower us we should remove them, by studying religious books and by reasoning. Religious books must not be treated like novels, to be read and put away on a book shelf. But they should be read, chewed and digested.

Meditation is not a one day affair. It is a process. For example if we are trying to break a large piece of stone using a chisel and a hammer, we strike hundred blows of the hammer on the stone through the chisel before the stone breaks. Were the ninety nine strokes a waste? So also we should not stop meditating after some practice for some months or one or two years. Even if we do a little practice, the effect is there. Nothing is lost. That is the immutable law of nature. So we must have unshakeable conviction in the existence of God and in the efficacy of meditation.

God helps those who help themselves. It is said that "If you walk four steps towards God, God will take eight steps towards you". So do not bother about doubts. There is no end for doubts. If we meditate regularly without any doubt, the doubts will be cleared in a mysterious manner.

Oil and metals are available in the bowels of the earth. But they are to be drilled, processed and purified. So also man has to undergo the process of purification. So we must patiently purify our mind. Till then we must never give up our attempt.

Nothing is permanent. Difficulties arise, but they pass away like water under the bridge. Give the suggestion to the mind. "Even this will pass away".

Jealousy:

Jealousy is the worst enemy of peace. One should rejoice in the welfare of others. Even some highly educated people are very mean and petty minded. Jealous people are far from God. So jealousy must be entirely rooted out.

Accepting Faults:

Some people never admit their faults and defects. Even if any one points out their defects for correcting them, they feel extremely annoyed. Sometimes they tell terrible, deliberate lies to defend them. Self justification is dangerous. But if a man wants to improve himself, he will begin to realize his faults. He will soon be on the direct road to correction and change himself.

Hatred:

Hatred is the deadliest foe. It is an inveterate enemy. A son hates his father; the father hates his son; A husband hates his wife—so on and so forth. Pure unselfish love should be cultivated. Hatred can be removed completely by realization of oneness of life. There is one Self hidden in all beings. Then why do we frown at others? Why do we treat others with contempt? Why do we divide and separate? Let us feel God everywhere. Rejoice and radiate love and peace everywhere.

Lower Nature:

We cannot lead a double life at the same time. Divine life cannot conform to little standards. We should rise above petty human level. We must kill all the lower nature attributes by developing high divine nature qualities and soar high. Let us remember that we are children of God. When meditation is practiced along with breathing exercises, the result is outstanding.

Man and the World:

Once the son of a business man irritated his father after he came home from a hectic day by asking many questions. The businessman in his anger tore out a world map and asked his son to set it right, to make the son engaged. He told his son that he would answer his questions later.

The son was intelligent. He knew that it was a difficult job. But he examined the torn map carefully. He found out that, behind the world map there was a picture of a man and so the boy just rearranged the bits and pieces of the man easily and made the picture of the man whole. By thus setting the 'Man' he set the 'World' and surprised his father. Likewise, if we set the man right (by killing his lower nature and developing the high divine nature) the world will be automatically set right. The world will always be what a man wants to make of it. Man is the cause and the world that he creates for himself is an effect.

Our planet is the only piece of real estate so far known in the universe. It is also true that human being is the most intelligent of the species in the planet, since he knows how to choose between two options. So it goes without saying that the future of the planet lies in his hands. Is he aware at all of his great responsibility?

33

Donkey

A donkey once fell into a pit. The master tried hard to bring up the donkey but in vain. So he ordered his servants to fill the pit with mud so that the donkey will be buried. The servants put some mud in the pit and the donkey treaded on the mud and came up. The servants again put some mud in the pit and the donkey again treaded on the mud and came up. The servants again put some mud in the pit and the donkey once again came up. In this manner the donkey came up and up repeatedly and finally came out of the pit.

Similarly the gloom of the world is but a shadow. Miseries are always blessings in disguise, because they purify our souls and take us nearer to God. The mother gives bitter medicine to her child, but it is for the welfare of the child. In everything we call a trial, a sorrow, an Angels hand is present. Life is so full of meaning and purpose-beneath its covering-that we will find earth that cloaks our heaven. Let our soul speak to us with the God-given wisdom it contains as a guide in our every thought and action. Accept everything, better or bitter because it has directly come from God.

The happiest man is he who brings out the best in him. The best in us is our divinity and the purpose of our life is to bring out our Divinity and be happy and enjoy Supreme bliss. There is no other short route for happiness.

Dear readers-please get over all the obstacles fearlessly one by one and manifest divine glory, splendor, purity and sanctity. Wait patiently with a calm and serene mind for results. Do not be hasty. Allow proper time for regeneration and renovation. Hold on to the banner of faith. March boldly and cheerfully. Be happy and radiate joy. Fulfill the Divine will.

Clarify yourselves and share these messages with your friends and dear ones. This noble and stupendous selfless work is awaiting you now in the grand plan. By reforming others we only reform ourselves. Thus we can make the world a better place to live in. Bless the whole world and the whole world will bless you.

34

Pain Killers

One of my friends was talking to me about his problems. He said, "Whenever I feel oppressed by my problems, I go to a wine shop. Once I have a drink, I forget all my cares and feel as if I am flying in the air. But what is the use? The moment my head clears, all my cares and problems return."

Let us see the other side of the story. My friend's children came to me and said, "Father comes home drunk and picks up a quarrel with mother. We are very unhappy about this. We don't like to be at home at all." My friend does not grudge spending money for his children's food, clothing and education. But all this expense appears to be a waste, because the children are not happy in that house. In short, the father has given his children everything except the most important thing, namely, peace and happiness. Hence he has failed in his duty as a father.

This is the situation in the homes of all liquor addicts. The father's habit of drinking not only affects the children's minds, but also serves to reduce their respect for the father who is simply not worried about the impact of his drunkenness on his children. The irony of the whole matter is that these liquor addicts do not want their children to take to liquor. Should the father not set a good example to his son?

Pain killers give only temporary relief from pain. They cannot get rid of the disease and effect a permanent cure. Drinking is not a solution to our problems. All human beings have problems. The only solution that can be followed by all men and women, is meditation. Our actions are the cause of all our problems. These actions are like a stain on the soul. Only meditation can remove this stain and provide relief from our sorrows. There is no short cut to happiness. No harm will be done by our going without food once. But not a day should pass without our doing meditation.

Liquor addicts should not forget that they are committing a sin when they fail to do their duty. Whenever you feel oppressed by sorrows, go to a temple, or sit before the picture of your favourite God and breathe deeply and slowly. As you breathe in, you can feel God's grace strength and kindness pervade your entire being. Meditate whole-heartedly. See how you derive peace of mind and spiritual strength. Meditation is the most powerful tonic. Let us not close all the doors and windows and say it is suffocating. There is air all around us. Yet you can blow air into a tyre only by means of a gas pump. In the same manner, God is everywhere. But we can realise him only through meditation. So, let us be courageous. Why should we be afraid of problems? Let us face the reality.

Body and soul

Drinks and drugs are worse than disease as they sap both body and soul. We do not provide facilities for thieves to indulge their propensity for thieving. Then why must the government facilitate drinking?

How to sit for meditation

Whether we sit or stand, our backbone should always be straight. We have seen soldiers standing erect. Only then our backbone is straight and energy is able to pass unobstructed through the backbone to the brain. When the backbone is bent, there is a block in the passage of energy to the brain. Moreover, when we sit upright, our lungs expand and the oxygen intake increases. In many parts of the world, oxygen bars have been set up and a situation has arisen in which we have to pay for the air we breathe.

Nowadays, many people suffer from worn out hip bones, shoulder bones etc., and therefore have to wear a waist belt, collar traction etc. Doctors say that those who sit upright do not suffer damage to their bones. Prevention is better than cure, is it not? When our mind is pure, it acquires unlimited power and we are able to achieve many things.

Aids to concentration

The easiest and the best way of worshipping God is hearing to devotional songs. There will be no tossing of mind. The various rays of the mind are collected and focused on God. Undoubtedly it is a pleasant experience. Try. If you are well-versed in music, you can sing to your hearts content. Singing easily elevates and expands mind. It also melts our mind and we become one with God.

We worship God by lighting lamps, candles etc., because we visualise God as light. We need light to dispel external and material darkness. But the same light dispels inner darkness also; that is, the light of knowledge removes the darkness of ignorance. When we meditate regularly without fail, our ignorance is removed. Saints who have seen God, have undergone a lot of suffering. But even in the midst of this adversity, they did not lose their faith in God. On the other hand, they surrendered themselves unconditionally to God. We should remember that they too found it difficult to bring their mind to concentrate to God.

This view is expressed humorously by the poet Thayumanavar. He says, "You can control a mad elephant. You can train lions, bears, tigers, snakes and so on. You can walk on water. You can bathe in fire. You can perform all kinds of miracles. But controlling the mind is the most difficult task of all." Saint Sankara voiced the same opinion, when he told God, "My mind is a monkey. Tie it with the string of devotion and keep it with you always." Although it is difficult to control the mind, if we are steadfast in our effort, it is possible to do it. Sunlight pervades the earth. But only when it is concentrated into a thin beam by means of a lens, it is capable of burning cotton. It is because the needle tip is sharp, that we are able to stitch our clothes with it. In the same manner, we should collect all our thoughts and concentrate them into one thin beam. This will give us immense power.

We should pray for others. Praying only for ourselves, is an incomplete act. If we pray for the welfare of everyone on earth, we also derive the benefit; and those around us are benefited too. Let us suppose for example, that an acquaintance of ours has been hospitalised for some illness. When we visit him, we find that he is writhing in pain. We feel terribly sorry for him, but we are unable to do anything to alleviate his pain. The patient needs a lot of courage and comfort to bear his pain. So we tell him, "Don't worry. You will get well soon. People who have been worse than you have recovered quite fast. I shall pray for you." This is all that we can do. But at that moment, those words are worth more than a crore of rupees. Once the patient realises that he is not alone in his suffering, that there are others to share it and console him, he derives fresh energy and confidence and recovers speedily. I have experienced this myself.

Charity does not mean monetary assistance alone. Words of comfort and confidence given to a needy person, is also charity of another kind. We should be willing to give money to people who need it for their medical expenses. If they need physical assistance, we should be willing to provide that also. We should seize opportunities like this to help people. We should remember that such good deeds alone will come to our aid if we are placed in a situation where we need help. Our relatives and friends may not be in a position to help us.

Alive even after death

Long after their death, my parents-in-law continue to live in the hearts of several people. They educated many people. They gifted their farmlands to the disabled. Generally, landlords, give only money to their labourers. But my father-in-law gave his farmhands free lunch (of good quality) and evening tea and snacks. Even strangers were welcome to the dining table. Money and materials were given ungrudgingly to all those who sought them. I am not writing this out of pride. This book will not be complete without a mention of my parents-in-law. Even now, people tell me,

"Your father-in-law's generosity will protect your family for years to come." The good live even after death.

Tagore's poem

Tagore is a world famous poet. He was the first Indian to win the Nobel Prize for literature. Let us read one of his poems.

I had a lot of grains in my bag. A man begged for alms. I gave him just two grains. Later, when I put my hands into my bag, I found that only two grains had turned into gold. I regretted that I had not given away all the grains.

This poem is found in The Gitanjali—a collection of Tagore's poems.

"He who giveth to the poor, lendeth to the Lord."

Similarly, when we pray for others, we are blessed by God. A selfish or undeserved request in prayer is rejected by the soul. Prayer, asking for forgiveness for misdeeds serves the purpose if the petitioner is sincere of cleansing his spirit.

35

Life Partner

Socrates' wife was very short-tempered and used to scold him off and on. Once she scolded and later on poured water upon him-Socrates referred to this as thunder and rain for he had a wonderful sense of humor. When once a young man asked his advice regarding marriage, Socrates advised him to get married. He said, 'If the wife is good, you will be happy. But if she is of a different temperament, then you will become a philosopher like me'.

The message is that if both husband and wife are spiritually oriented, which is indeed a rare blessing, there is no difficulty. If, however, one is not spiritually inclined, it might further increase the devotion. One must pray intensely to God to show the path. He may graciously turn the mind of the spouse favorably or may give strength to the spiritually inclined spouse to withdraw from the world internally or externally even. Cases are known where chaste and spiritually inclined wives have transformed their sensuous husbands into saintly personalities.

36

Be not afraid of sorrow

It is only when misfortunes continue to befall us, that our faith in God either decreases or is lost completely. What is the use of being good? what avails meditation? we ask. Your doubts will vanish after you read this chapter and you will be wiser.

- Joy and sorrow are natural in this world
- This world is full of opposites.

For example:

concave	x	convex
man	x	woman
day	x	night
negative	x	positive
North pole	x	South pole
beauty	x	ugliness

Hence, joy and sorrow are a part of life.

- Only in sorrow we realise the value of joy. We learn through adversity. This knowledge prevents us from repeating our mistakes.

- Sorrow chastens us, shapes us. God gives us periodical pinpricks, so that we gain knowledge, wisdom and completeness. God tests us to see whether we are sincere and straight forward even in sorrow and poverty. This is the link between God and us. We are constantly moving towards perfection. "Blessed are the pure in heart, for they shall see God."

- Do not grieve that you are beset with misfortunes, that there is no progress in your life. Only when we are halfway through the river, we can see the other bank. When crossing the ocean, we cannot see any shore. It is ignorance to say that God does not exist, when we are in sorrow.

- Continuing to grieve is not a solution to problems. Readers, please understand this properly. In a crisis, or when misfortune strikes, let us not lament about what has happened. Instead, let us say, "Alright. What is past, is past. How shall we remedy this?" That alone will be prudent. Successful people will agree with me. The proprietor of the famous Ford Company, Henry Ford, used to tell his employees, "Don't find fault; find the remedy."

What should be done in adversity

Problems which cause sorrow, are of two kinds. Some problems can be solved by us. We should study such problems, find their causes and then find the solutions to them as best as we can. Some problems defy 'human' solutions. In such cases, it is better to leave things to God and abide by His will peacefully. A story will make this clear. A villager was travelling by train. He had goods that weighted ten kg. The TTR came to him and said, "You are permitted to have only 5kg. of goods. Since you have an excess of 5 kg., you must pay fine." The villager replied, "I shall carry the excess 5kg. on my head". "The TTR said, "O fool, whether you carry the load on your head or in your hands, it is the train which bears the burden." It is up to us to do our duty. If we leave the rest to God, we can be at peace. This does not mean that we should sit back and say, "God created us and therefore He will take care of us." God helps only those who help themselves. Cosmic energy is an autonomous energy. When we make an attempt to achieve something, cosmic energy will assist us in our endeavor. There is a time to be active and there is a time to be inactive. Time solves many problems.

"IF ONLY"—The two saddest words in any language.

37

Why does prayer not give immediate relief from suffering?

We say that meditation relieves sorrow. But sometimes even good people who meditate regularly, are subjected to pain and sorrow. If it is possible to obtain relief through meditation immediately then men will commit all kinds of crimes and seek redress through meditation. And if God forgives such men, then crimes will increase. Nature dictates that perpetrators of crimes should experience the same agony that their victims experienced. That is why criminals are punished. But we need not worry. The future lies ahead of us. Meditation will relieve our suffering, **slowly** but **surely**. We have a long way to go. If the evil surrounding us is compared to a forest, meditation can be compared to an axe that can cut down the trees in the forest. It may take time to cut down the trees, but it is possible to clear the forest in course of time. God is not impatient. He has given us endless time and space in which to work out our destiny.

Why do the good suffer?

People may be good now. But their past follows them. What they experience in this birth, is the result of their actions in their previous birth.

The sum of all our past deeds, is called 'Sanjitha Karma'.

What we have experienced already in our present birth, is called 'Praptha'.

What remains to be experienced, is called 'Aagaamiya Karma'.

Only after we have experienced all this, can we attain salvation and see God. Until then, we may have to continue to suffer. All evil has to be banished.

Till then we have to wait patiently. We cannot jump from kindergotton into high school. God and nature are not in a hurry. The rewards of spiritual growth are certain and unfailing. Nothing our soul has really gained can ever be taken away from it.

There is one important point that we must remember in this regard.

Just as we now suffer for our past misdeeds, we may have to suffer in the future for our present misdeeds. You cannot sow weeds and hope to reap grains. Intelligent people will be afraid of sinning. We go to temples only to purify ourselves. If we continue to sin, it is equal to having a bath and then falling into drain. We cannot change the past. Let us therefore start a new life from today. Let today be the first day of a fresh life—devoid of sin. A bright future awaits all good people. Wicked people may appear to be happy now, because of some good deeds done in the past. But when they begin to suffer for their wicked deeds, nobody can do anything to prevent their suffering.

How do those who have seen God describe their joy?

Those who have seen God wish to describe their bliss, but words fail them. They cannot remain silent also, because they want others to share their happiness. They say that even all the joy in this world put together cannot equal their joy in seeing God.

38

Why are wishes not fulfilled?

Many people request God to grant them this and that. Some of their requests are granted; some are not. When they do not get what they asked for, they are disappointed. This is due to ignorance. We must have a clear cut idea about this. Good men go to temples; bad men also go to temples. Who will God bless?

Formula

What we are at this moment, is the result of the sum total of our past deeds.

Life = All our good deeds + all our bad deeds + our meditation in full.

These three entities determine our life.

All of us have a past history. There is a law which governs the entire universe. Similarly there is a law governing meditation. According to that law, our past deeds determine what the results of our meditation should be. Without realising this truth, we should not say, "I prayed for so long, but I did not get any reward." God cannot be measured with a measuring tape.

There are several patients in a hospital. The doctor advises some of them to eat well; some of them to diet. Some of them are advised complete rest; some are advised to exercise. Some are given only tablets; some are operated upon. The treatment given to the patients depends on their illness. The doctor is the same. Prolonged illness requires prolonged treatment. In the same way, God blesses each one of us according to our deeds. Let us not lament that meditation has not fetched us any reward. God can see even a small ant moving. Sometimes we meditate with a particular goal in view. But we are rewarded in a different manner. The ultimate truth is that, God always gives us more than what we expect. He has a master-plan for us. This may sometimes work out slowly. But it will work.

Hence, whatever God has given us—wealth, children, parents, spouse, beauty, education—we have merited as our earning. Our mind is a storehouse of thoughts. Let us keep it clean. Let us not lament saying, "This is my fate." Jesus said that if we wish, we can be gods. Let us, therefore, try to fashion our fate anew.

God is omniscient

We know only the past and the present. But God knows the past, present and future. God arranges our present to suit our future.

A student who stays in a hostel, has to abide by its rules and regulations, which he may not relish now. But the discipline and self-control which he practices now, will stand him in good stead in the future. A mother gives her child bitter medicine only for its own good.

Nature heals

Whatever be the condition, there is no need for us to lose heart because God is full of mercy to his children. For example, nature always heals. Suppose we cut our figures, nature gives new cells, tissues and new skin.

Even before we were born we were cared for and protected by God, the Father of all things. Can we doubt that this care and protection and creative provision will be any less in the boundless eternity ahead?

The gloom of the world is but a shadow. Life is so generous a giver and in everything we call a trial or sorrow, let us believe that Angel's hand is there.

39

The Will of God

Once there was a village in which there was a very honest devout weaver. He would preface every statement with "By the will of God"

Everyone knew how honest he was because in selling a piece of cloth, he would tell the price he paid for the cloth, how much he charges for the labor and how much his profit will be, prefacing each of these "by the will of God".

One day he was in the temple praying and contemplating, when some thieves came by. They had just committed a robbery and they needed someone to carry a lot. Seeing the weaver sitting alone in the temple they grabbed him and put the bundle of loot on his head and asked him to walk with them. The police arrived and arrested everyone including the weaver. When he was produced in front of the magistrate and asked to explain what happened, he said, "By the will of God, I was sitting in the temple. By the will of God the thieves came and made me carry their loot. By the will of God I am now in front of you".

Thus even in these circumstances he did not lose his peace of mind or develop any anxiety, because it was all the will of God. The magistrate was convinced of his honesty and released him and he told his friends "By the will of God I am released".

If we can have that kind of self surrender, we will never be assailed by worry or anxiety. To reach that level of self surrender, we must remember the fact that whatever has a beginning has an ending. The problems we are facing now had a beginning and they will have an ending. No problem lasts forever.

Worrying about a problem will not help us to solve it, and that all we can do it is to try out best.

40

Salt merchant (Blessing in disguise)

Once there lived a salt merchant. He used to load his asses with sacks of salt, take them to the shandy (market) and sell the salt there. On the way he had to pass through a forest. One day, soon after he entered the forest, it began to rain. The salt was dissolved in the rain water. The merchant was very angry with God for having deprived him of his profit that day. He returned home awfully disappointed.

After some time he saw people gathering in groups and talking about something seriously. He learnt that a gang of robbers had been seen in the forest that day. They had planned to rob (at gun point) the merchants returning from the shandy. The merchant now felt sorry for having been angry with God for sending down rain. Had it not rained, he may have been killed by the robbers while returning. God gives us small losses which are, in reality, precursors to big gains. Hence, we should be happy with whatever God gives us.

Life is so full of meaning and purpose, that we can discern God's hand even in what appear to us to be trials or sorrows.

41

Guru and disciple

There are many guru and disciple stories that teach us valuable lessons. Once there lived a guru and disciple. Everyday, they used to go from house to house, beg for food and eat it. At other times they would go to the temple and worship God. The guru taught his disciple, "You should never say that God has not given you anything. God always gives us everything." The disciple listened to this carefully. One night, the guru and the disciple did not get anything for food. They returned to the pyol where they usually went to bed. The guru got ready to sleep. But the disciple was very hungry and was not prepared to sleep. So he asked his guru, "Guruji, you said I should never say that God has not given us anything. But tonight I am forced to say so, because God has really not given us anything to eat."

The guru laughed and said, "What I told you is still true. God has given us life. He has given us this pyol to sleep. He has given us a healthy body and powerful limbs. He has given us hunger also." The disciple realised his mistake and said, "Yes, God has given us everything."

Many incidents take place in our lives. In fact, life is a collection of incidents. If we observe life carefully, we will find that these incidents are closely linked to one another. For example, we learnt to write when we were about four years old. That practice helps us to write even now. In other words, what happened when we were four years old, is linked to what is happening now. All the incidents are linked in such a way that they form a chain. It is not possible to remove or change one of those links.

Suppose ten people participate in a running race. If all of them pray to God that they should get the first prize, is it possible? One man's victory is another man's failure. We learn from these examples, that nature will takes its own course. We cannot and should not meddle with it.

"When you are discouraged thinking all is lost
Count your many blessings, name them only be one,"

42

Tackling problems with a positive outlook

All the disciples were gathered around Buddha to hear his sermons on the right way to live. However, on this particular day, Buddha did not preach—instead, he announced, "Most of you here have been with me for more than 5 years. You have lived an austere life and heard me speak on various topics time and again. I feel that it is time for some of you to go across the country, and spread my teachings far and wide. Today, I would like to evaluate some of you, to see if you have attained the maturity to represent me, my beliefs and my teachings to the larger community".

This would indeed be an honor, the disciples thought. Each of them eagerly awaited their turn to meet Buddha and have a discussion with him. One after the other, they met Buddha alone, but came back with sad faces because they had not answered his questions to his satisfaction.

Finally, it was the turn of one of Buddha's most devoted disciples. When he approached Buddha, Buddha asked him to sit in a relaxed manner, give calm thought to his questions and respond in the manner the disciple felt was appropriate.

Buddha asked his first question. "Suppose I choose you to represent me and spread my teachings. You reach a village and when the villagers assemble around you, you start sharing these lessons. But the villagers laugh and mock you, scold you and chase you away from the village. What would you do?"

The disciple thought for a moment, and then responded, "I would consider myself fortunate that they only verbally assaulted me and that I had been spared any physical pain. I would move on to the next village and start again".

Buddha smiled and said, "When you reach the second village, and you start your sermons, the villagers again jeer and call out rude names. A few of them also start hitting you until you start bleeding. What would you do now?".

The disciple pondered a few minutes and then replied, "I would consider myself blessed that though they had hurt me, they had not killed me. I would move on to the next village and start afresh on spreading your teachings".

Buddha now asked seriously, "What if this is a village of ruthlessly violent people, who do not spare a thought to your teachings but instead start attacking you until you breathe your last?".

The disciple did not hesitate as he answered, "Master, life in this world is filled with problems and suffering. I will consider myself freed from this tortuous life and a step closer to eternal salvation".

Buddha laid his hand on the disciple's head and said, "My son, you have learnt well as a student and attained the maturity needed to become a teacher. Go forth into the world and spread my teachings on right living. My blessings will go with you".

Thus, we learn from this story, that facing problems with a positive attitude will help us to move from suffering to peace. We need to practice always looking for the good in every situation. Let us keep in mind that every cloud has a silver lining, and when we focus on the positive, the negative effects will shrink in comparison and lose the power to intimidate and control us.

43

What to do when in unbearable pain?

We should not think only about ourselves. We should remember that many others having bigger problems, have overcome them and been successful. Umpteen examples can be given; but the best seems to be that of Helen Keller. As a child, she was deaf and dumb and blind. Can anything be worse than this? For all practical purposes, she was almost dead. In fact, neighbours even suggested to Helen's mother to put her to death. But the mother employed a teacher to teach Helen. How can a deaf and blind child be taught? The teacher, however, was as remarkable as Helen herself. Untiringly, she took to teaching the child. She took Helen to a tap, let the water flow through her fingers and then wrote the word 'water' on her palm. She repeated this several times. Sometimes, the teacher allowed Helen to feel her throat, her lips and even her tongue while she talked. Thus Helen learnt many things.

Later Helen completed her college education using the Braille method. She wrote some great novels and became world famous. Not content with this, she travelled all over the world and raised funds for the disabled. She addressed people, exhorting them to be always cheerful. What she spoke was intelligible only to her teacher, who translated her 'speech' to the listeners. Having lived a very successful life despite multiple handicaps, Helen Keller passed away peacefully in her sleep at the ripe old age of 84. Hence we should learn to count our blessings and be thankful for them always. Whenever you feel depressed that all is lost, think how blessed you have been compared to others. All of us are born to achieve something. All of us have some talent or the other. Try to make full use of it and progress in life.

44

What is the purpose of our birth?

Only through meditation can we gradually reduce our sorrows. But we must have the patience to wait. We must wait for the cosmic law to function right. God has given us cotton. Making clothes is our duty. There is a proverb which says, "Clever men have blankets. Leggards (lazy men) have only sheep."

In a certain town, there once lived a rich man. He employed a rustic as his servant. One day, he sent the servant to the nearby city to buy some things. The rustic had never seen a city before. Hence he was overawed by the grand shops and decorative lights. He simply stood there, admiring the sights. He forgot the purpose of his visit and did not buy anything. Many of us are like the rustic in this story. God has created us to do our duty, meditate and achieve lofty goals. But the majority of us forget our ideals and indulge in worldly pleasures. Let us lay down new codes for ourselves.

"We are not here to play, to dream and to drift,
We have hard work to do and loads to fight."

Let us remove the stains from our soul. Let us make sure that fresh stains do not taint our soul.

45

All religions are one

When we were in Madurai, we had two Christian families as our neighbours. They would give us cakes and sweets for Christmas and New year. Similarly, we would give them sweets, sugarcane and tubers for Deepavali and Pongal. They used to treat me as their daughter.

As I had my schooling in a convent, I am familiar with Christ's teachings. The Christian codes and precepts that we were taught in school, are very similar to Hindu codes and precepts. As students, all of us would gather in the school chapel and kneel and pray. Seeing the serene face of Jesus gave us a certain peace of mind. Did He not say, "When somebody hits you on one cheek, show him the other?" Even now, we have a statue of Mother Mary of Velankanni in our pooja room. The receipts laid down in the Koran, are also admirable.

In recent times there have been several religious and caste clashes which are very unfortunate and mentally disturbing. The sole reason for these clashes, is ignorance. These clashes occur only among uneducated people. Educating them is the only solution.

1. There is only one God
2. As God dwells in all living beings, we should love all of them
3. A man who does not respect another man following a different religion, cannot be said to respect his own religion
4. All religions preach only good

Those who have learnt these truths, must teach them to others.

The manner in which Christians and Muslims kneel and pray, provides good exercise to the body. Similarly the way in which Hindus prostrate and pray to lord Ganesha, gives good exercise to the body. When Ayyappa devotees chant "Swamiye Saranam Ayyappa" it is an excellent breathing exercise as the chanting involves deep breathing. Such exercises prevent many diseases. All religions advocate several precepts that are good for everyone. We should learn and accept them.

Why worship idols?

An unknown number (in Mathematics) is referred to as 'X'—Infinity is also X. God is omnipresent. But because we cannot refer to Him as X, we give Him a form and worship Him in that form. Once we have rid ourselves of all our past good and bad, we shall certainly see God. Until such time, we need to worship him in a particular form.

A mother knows what kind of food her child likes. So she prepares only what he likes. In the same way, God knows how his devotee worships Him, and He manifests Himself in that form to his devotee. Whether we are Hindus, Muslims or Christians, let us try to be true Hindus, true Muslims and true Christians. Although all religions preach alike, we are accustomed to a particular form of worship right from childhood, and prefer to follow the same. Just as temple tower, a church steeple and the dome of a darga rise high into the sky, our minds should also rise high and majestic.

46

The illiterate are blind

Once there lived a king. A poor scholar came to the king and requested him to alleviate his poverty. The king felt very sorry for the scholar. Hence he wished to give him sufficient monetary assistance. He gave him some money initially and asked him to come again the next day. The scholar came the next day. The king told the scholar to walk along a particular path. The scholar obeyed the king's orders. He found that it was a broad avenue with flowering trees on either side. The scholar was fascinated by the beauty of the path. Then an idea struck him. He thought to himself, "Why not I walk with my eyes closed? There are no potholes here." Hence he closed his eyes and walked forward. The king had left a bundle of gold coins in the middle of the road for the scholar to pick up. But the scholar missed the bundle and went home. Thus we sometimes become blind because we have eyes that see not.

Here is another example. Uneducated people sometimes do not even know what is good and what is bad. There is no limit to the foolishness of their actions. Recently, an incident took place in a village called Satpura in Uttar Pradesh. A man called Maheesha died. His wife Shansha was forced to commit 'sati' by burning herself on her husband's funeral pyre. She was given a ceremonial bath, decked like a bride and then pushed into the fire. The villagers foolishness did not stop there.

Members of her family claimed that she had died at the behest of Goddess Durga, and that all their problems would be solved if a temple were to be erected at the site of her death. To this end, they began collecting money from everyone around. Can there be anything more idiotic than this?

Even this, is nothing compared to female infanticide and child marriages—especially the marriage of a seven-year-old girl with a fifty year-old man. Despite great strides in scientific progress, there is large scale ignorance and illiteracy. Today, women have proved themselves equal to men in all fields; but girl babies continue to be killed. Isn't this atrocious?

Because I happen to live in a village, I have had the experience of observing villagers. The majority of them are illiterate. Hence they are steeped in ignorance. So, when I talk to them about spiritual matters, they are not able to understand such things. It is their inability to reason and discriminate that leads them to fake religious leaders and to be deceived by cheats. It is their ignorance that leads them to wrong-doing. Isn't this a great tragedy?

We can never be said to have progressed fully, as long as there is illiteracy amidst us. Only if education—especially education combined with spirituality—is made legally compulsory in all the countries of the world, can we have a crimeless society. Until then, people will continue to commit mistakes and as a result create problems and tension for themselves. The establishment of a crimeless society alone, will warrant true millennium celebrations. There is no other solution for the present state of affairs.

47

The only way

Today, the whole world is afflicted by militancy and violence. All the countries are trying to find out ways of combating this evil. But the prospects of finding a way out seem to be bleak. The fault lies in our educational system. UNLESS THAT SYSTEM IS ALTERED THERE CAN BE NO REDEMPTION.

Just reflect a while. Every parent wishes that his child should become a doctor, an engineer or a teacher. So he sends his child to a school that he thinks will educate him accordingly. These schools or institutions also educate their students in the best manner possible. But is there any school or college that teaches a person to be 'human'? Only if spiritual education based on science is imparted, good students can be produced and a good society established.

Children should be taught that they should never do wrong under any circumstances. They should be afraid to do wrong and feel guilty if they violate the rules of good conduct. In short, every cell in our body should be injected with good qualities. Catch them young, should be the watchword. Unless the fear of God is instilled in the minds of the young, they can never be corrected in their later life.

I would like to give an example from my own experience. One day I had gone to a shop. Some students also came there. The shopkeeper was an elderly man and appeared to be quite poor. His life depended on the profit he made from selling goods in that shop. He had displayed greeting cards on one side and fancy items on the other side in his shop. While he was selling greeting cards to the customers, some of the students stole bangles and hid them in their dress. When he turned to sell the fancy goods, the students stole the greeting cards and put them in their bags. I was shocked when I saw this. If educated youngsters behave like this, what will the uneducated youth do? What was the use of their education? The fault lies not with the students, but with the system. Had they been taught ethics and sound moral values early in their life, would their conscience not have warned them that they were doing wrong?

In ancient times, the 'Gurukula' system of education prevailed in India. This system included spiritual education. Society then was good. In course of time, that system changed. Tagore, however, founded Shantiniketan where the Gurukula system was practised. It is worth mentioning that Nehru sent his daughter Indira Gandhi to Shantiniketan recognizing the merits of the system followed there.

Those who have not been given moral education are like people who have eyes that see not. Society is made up of individuals. If the individual are good society will be good. Self perfection leads to world perfection. If the foundation is strong, the super structure will also be strong. Only a strong foundation of moral education given to the child when young, will help him to lead a pure life when he grows up.

"A fine thread will control an honest man better than a strong rope will do the rogue."

Let us assume that a huge fire destroys an entire forest. Within a short time all the trees will grow again, because the fire does not destroy the roots of the trees. Similarly, all the evil in this world can be destroyed only by a change in the mental attitude of men.

48

Mother

Just as a fish feels at home in water, likewise a baby feels very happy and comfortable in a holy and divine atmosphere. When the mother constantly thinks of God and prays wholeheartedly for her child's wellbeing, the child swims in an ocean of bliss. The child feels happy if the mother treats it as a sacred gift of God. It feels great joy when the mother lovingly embraces it and holds it to her bosom in a warm embrace. All these positive feelings and vibration strengthen the inner power of the child.

Even before the birth of the child, the parents should have lofty thoughts. An expecting mother is advised to read epics and religious books to bring forth healthy and strong children with a very good character.

A mother's lap is the child's first school. Children learn so many important things from their mother. This learning is not just from the things she explains to them, but from the way she lives her life. Example is the most powerful and lasting lesson parents can give to a child. A chain smoker cannot advise his son to give up smoking!

Here is a small anecdote. A physician prescribed medicine for a patient. He said to him, "Come another day and I'll give you directions about diet." The physician had several jars of molasses in his room that day. The patient lived very far away. He visited the physician another day and the physician said to him, "Be careful about your food. It is not good for you to eat molasses". After the patient left, another person who was there asked the physician, "The patient lives far away and why did you give him the trouble of coming here again. You could have very well given the instructions about food the first day itself?" The physician replied with a smile, "There is a reason. I had several jars of molasses in my room that day. If I had asked the patient that day to give up molasses, he would have not have had faith in my words. He would have thought, "He has so many jars of molasses in his room, he must eat some of it. Then molasses can't be so bad". Today I have hidden all the jars. So now he will have faith in my words".

The moral of the story is: it is the example that matters most. Every teacher and parents should bear this in mind. Children learn so many things from their mothers. If the mother is patient, the child is also patient. A child should be encouraged to practice virtues like honesty, tolerance, sprit of compassion, sacrificing for the good of others, caring and sharing and straight forwardness. Thus the mother should properly mould the mind and character of the child. If not, what the mother does not only harms the child but also the child's child. It is well said that "The hand that rocks the cradle rules the world.

An honest child will never indulge in bribery throughout his life. Bribery is basically stealing through intimidation. The able bodied beggar demanding alms on the street is no different from the able bodied businessman who uses his positions to exact payments not due. If a child is not taught to honest, he will not become a true citizen. A healthy society is based on honesty, trust, love and goodwill. So it is all in the hands of the mother. The future of the society lies solely in the hands of the mother.

Religion begins in the home. The mother goes to the temple to get strong. She goes to the temple to draw strength from God and returns home where she maintains a similar vibration in which to raise the next generation to be wonderfully productive citizens of the world, to bring peace on earth. The atmosphere at home matters most. Children should be exposed to spiritual education. If not the school cannot teach religious tolerance and love of humanity.

"Lives of great men all remind us; we can make our life sublime". Parents should always remind the children of the lives of great men. "Home is the first school".

"Let your mother be a God". "Let your father be God".

The parents should bear in mind what a responsibility it is to be worthy of such a stature.

Unfortunately, in modern days, parents leave their children under the care of paid servants. On account of this, children consider themselves neglected and negative attitudes sink into the child's mind. This negligence and lack of affection makes the child psychologically and emotionally insecure. What will the next generation be like if the children are raised under such circumstances? Will it be strong and self assured? Will it radiate kindness to others never having had kindness given to it? It is a proven fact that most prison inmates were seriously neglected or beaten as children.

It is also a proven fact that all parents who mistreat their children were themselves mistreated by their parents. So in turn they raise their children in the same manner, for that is the only example of parenthood they have. So they think that neglect is natural. It's a cycle. A childhood of neglect produces bitter adult life and terrorist are such examples.

Here is a story of a neglected child. Raju was a ten year old boy, full of understanding and affection. His father worked as a lawyer. He was working very hard and was always busy with the litigation work. So he could not find time to spend some happy moments with his only son. Raju longed for the company of his father. He had been disappointed that his father did not attend the parents meet at his school.

One evening Raju interrupted his father and asked him, "Daddy how much does a good advocate earn in one hour" His father said with great reservation "See my dear boy, I charge five hundred rupees per hour". Raju was surprised that an hour of his father costs so much. However he seemed to calculate within himself for a while and then asked his father, "Daddy, I have saved five hundred rupees. Will you sell me an hour of your time, so that you can come to my school on Friday?" Father was moved to tears.

Like Raju's father, many modern parents face a very difficult challenge. But if parents do not arrange their lives to be there for their children they will regret it and after it's too late, so will the society.

49

The Best Way to Teach Peace

What is the best way to teach peace to the world? The best way is to first teach families to be peaceful within their home. Humans do not have horns or claws; nor do they have sharp teeth. Their weapon is their intelligence. Humans are essentially instinctive and intellectual. The instinctive nature is based on good and bad. But the soul nature is based on oneness, humility, peace, compassion love and helpfulness. The intellectual nature is based on trying to figure out both of these two. It works out formulas, finds solutions and processes knowledge. The key is meditation, yoking the energies of the soul with the energies of the body and yoking the energies of the soul with the energies of the mind. Then one becomes conscious in the soul. Now the soulful qualities are unfolded and a man is filled will divine love.

Children must be taught through the examples of parents and by learning the undiniable facts of life, the basic tenets that an all pervasive force holds this universe together, that we create with this force every minute, every hour, every day and because time is a cycle, what we create comes back to us. Once they learn this, they are winners. It is up to the parents to create the peace makers of the future. A home where love abides is truly a home. Otherwise it can be called only a building with four walls made up of bricks!

Nevertheless, we see society learning itself apart through retaliation. Countries divide and retaliate. To retaliate means to pay back injury with injury, to return like for like, evil for evil, an eye for an eye and a tooth for a tooth. It seems to be a part of human being, though it is a negative part of human kind. It does not have to prevail. It is not spiritual. It is demonic, a wrong use of will power. But we must remember, the force will come back on them three times stronger than they gave it out, because their strong will power will bring it back with vigor. This is the law. They will fall into pit of remorse and depression.

It is said that "Worthless are those who injure others, while those who stoically endure are like stored gold. Just as the earth bears those who dig into her, it is best to bear with those who despise us" We cannot hurt others without getting hurt back in the future. The wise person chooses his action according to this law.

Some might ask, "Does non-retalation mean that one should not protect himself, his family, his community. We are talking about revenge, not self-defence. Forgiving others is good. But if the matter is a serious one, we can seek reconciliation through the laws of the land. In criminal cases justice can be sought through the courts. It is not wise to take matters into our own hands and be the instrument of punishment, for by doing so we reap the same negative consequences as the offender. Retaliation on a wide scale can be seen in cases of mob violence and terrorism. Therefore it is wise to teach everybody about this law and to cultivate the powerful force of compassion, of righteous response, forgiveness, of admitting our own mistakes, of not lying our way out of a situation just to make ourselves look good, or putting others down.

All these virtues should also be taught in schools. Unfortunately education does not equip to handle these issues. Our education is chiefly concerned with studying the objective universe. Most of our present education, is data based, object based and prepares us only to earn more money, enjoy more and be competitive and live a fast paced life.

Education is not the amount of information we put into our brain and run riot there, undigested all our lives. But it should be life building, man making, character making and assimilations of ideas. If we have assimilated these ideas and made them our life and character, we have more education than any man who has by heart a whole library.

50

Life Education

Once a very well-versed scholar was traveling in a boat that took people from one side of a full flowing river to the other side. The people who traveled with him were not so learned as he. The scholar wanted to show off his knowledge and was asking the man who sat near him if he knew about Shelley and Keats. When the man replied in the negative, the scholar exclaimed that he had wasted half his life.

Suddenly the boatman asked the scholar if the knew swimming. The scholar replied that he did not know swimming. The boatman said at once that his whole life was wasted as the boat was about to sink due to a leakage. Everyone of the passengers swam safely while the scholar was drowned. That is the fate of the people who are deprived of a complete education. That means education that does not teach virtues like self-discipline, unselfishness, patience, love and morality.

Education must help to swim across the ocean of life. Education must help us to face all the situations in a righteous manner.

51

The soft-heartedness of children

One can see a new awareness among school children. Many of them refrain from buying crackers for Diwali. "Our conscience does not permit us to burst crackers prepared by children like us under dangerous conditions", they say. They add, "Innumerable children are deprived of school education, and sent to work in factories. They look at us going to school with longing. All this makes us sad. Even celebrating Children's Day all by ourselves, seems meaningless."

All over the world today, millions of children go to work. Governments should alleviate their poverty and give them good education. That alone will pave the way for a good society.

Hence, moral philosophy should be made a compulsory subject in schools all over the world.

52

Why do governments fail to do good?

Politicians have to spend several millions of rupees to contest and win an election. Hence, once they are elected, their first job is to recover all the money that they spent during the elections. Thus they are not able to implement any scheme that will benefit the people. They indulge in glorifying themselves and criticising their opponents. A politician comes to power only by winning the majority votes. His primary concern, therefore, should be to do good to those who voted him to power. Moreover, if a politician does not possess the virtues of simplicity, integrity and sincerity, he will earn the ill-will of the people. Those who do not give good governance, will certainly be punished by law or by God.

Not only politicians but bureaucrats too, must be straight forward and duty—conscious. Otherwise, no government schemes can be implemented properly. The advent of television has enabled even uneducated people know all about politics and politicians.

Every country in the world should impart education that is based on spirituality. Only then can militancy and terrorism be eradicated. Mentally healthy people can alone constitute a nation's strength. Nothing can be achieved without this.

There is no point in people waiting for the day when politicians and bureaucrats will turn a new leaf. Remember they are our representatives. First of all we should change. Society is made up of individuals. If these individuals are good, society will be good. We cannot expect governments or churches, made up human beings, to save mankind, until man himself, through right thinking, brings about his own salvation.

53

Read books

Do you yearn to make a mark in life? Read on. A life sans goals is a ship without a captain. Read the biographies of great men. Read the lives of men who began from scratch; men trodden upon by others; men who, despite all odds rose to great heights. Only then will we understand the sufferings they underwent and the problems they faced. Only then will we be inspired to set ourselves high goals. Reading books is a good hobby, because, as Dr. Radhakrishnan said, "When you read good books your thoughts also become noble." (And whenever you wish to gift something to somebody buy books and give them). Books make great gifts as well.

Our mind should be like a parachute. Only when it is open, it is useful. So keep the mind receptive to new ideas. Reading is a pleasant pastime. "Reading maketh a complete man."

Mr. Annadurai was once the Chief Minister of Tamil Nadu. He was a genius. He was well-read. Stricken by cancer, he was admitted into a hospital. It was decided that he had to be operated upon. But Annadurai requested his doctor to postpone the operation by two days. When the doctor asked him the reason, Annadurai replied that he was reading an important philosophical book and he would like to complete it before death overcame him.

Good books are like beacon lights to us, whenever we feel depressed or lost. They lead us forward and are like a balm to our fevered souls.

"Books are masters who instruct us without rods."
—Richard De Bury.

"The books that help you most are those
which make you think most."
—T.Parker.

"That is a good book which is opened with expectation
and closed with delight and profit."
—A.B.Alcott.

54

The mahout and the elephant

In a certain town there was a guru. He had a disciple. The guru had taught his disciple that God dwelt in every living being. One day, the disciple was walking along the road, when he saw an elephant coming towards him. Immediately, he remembered his guru's words, "God dwells in every living being". "That means God is in me; and God is in the elephant also. That God will not harm this God," he said to himself and went very close to the animal. The elephant lifted him with his trunk, whirled him in the air and threw him down. Luckily, he fell on a haystack and was saved. But he was badly shaken, because he did not expect that the elephant would treat him thus.

So he went straight to his guru and narrated the incident in detail. He asked the guru accusingly, "You only said that God dwelt in every living being. Why then did the elephant throw me like this?" The guru laughed and said, "What I said is true. Was the mahout not on the elephant? There is a God in him also. Did he not warn you not to come too close to the elephant? Why didn't you listen to his warning?"

Many of us are like the disciple in this story. He came to grief because he did not heed the mahout's warning. We also suffer because we do not pay heed to what the Scriptures say. No religion advocates murder, robbery, adulteration, corruption and deception. But people practise all these crimes brazenly and visit temples and pray to God. Why do we indulge in this hypocrisy? Let us reason things. God rewards only those who deserve them (rewards). Let us think wisely and act wisely. Let us produce good citizens who will make up a good society.

God is not a magician to give us all that we ask for. Religion is not a question of following a particular creed or attending a church. The true value of worship lies in our mental attitude and not in outward action. Those who do not follow the precepts laid down by the Scriptures, are like the disciple in the story. Mere outward forms of worship are useless, as long as our minds remain impure. Hence, when we do not follow the path of righteousness, buying all the flowers in the world and offering them to God, will fetch us no good. Let us not be beggars. Those who do not ask anything for themselves, are the richest. They have an abundance of love, life and strength to give to others. We are surrounded by truth and truth alone.

But the tragedy of the whole matter is that even educated people are like the disciple in the story. Believing in God is actually believing in goodness. That is, believing that God will reward those who are good. Today, people believe that even if you commit all kinds of sins, once you go to a temple and pray to God, He will reward you. Be a producer, not a prisoner of such an idiotic society!

Dear friends! Do not allow the cataract of ignorance to blur your vision. Remove it immediately and put on a new set of glasses—of wisdom. Let us be alert. Those who err, are like the blind searching for a black cat in a dark room.

It is like the blind leading the blind. "Man's good fortune and misfortune are not predestined; he brings them on himself by his conduct. The consequences of good and bad follows, as the shadow follows the body."

—*Kan Ying Phein*

Signposts

Just as when we do not know the way to some place, we require the assistance of a guide, similarly we need the help of saints to show us the way to a better understanding of the whole scheme of life. If we rely wholly on ourselves to find our way, we may take a circuitous route. This is where saints come to hlep mankind. Their whole life is a voluntary sacrifice for the good of humanity and so we can trust them.

They are not like novels

Do not treat scriptures like novels which you read once and discard. Scriptures should be read, chewed and digested. They don't mean anything unless we live them. They are not to be put away on the shelf. They are real only when we follow them. Otherwise they remain mere books to us.

The influence of a spiritual character

When we follow the teachings of the saints sincerely, we realise our own divine heritage and we are able to take our stand as worthy children of God. Thus we bless ourselves and help others also. Just think of the influence of a spiritual character on others! It lasts for ages. The message which the Buddha gave five hundred years before the Christian era, still lives.

55

Must we renounce everything?

People believe that spirituality implies renouncing everything. A spiritual life does not demand that we give up everything. We give up nothing but we only fill everything with richness of feeling and with idealistic thoughts. One who showers his love on others, is a spiritualist. One who possesses good qualities, is a spiritualist. One who performs his duties well, is a spiritualist. One who helps others is a spiritualist. Spirituality helps our virtues to shine through daily mediation.

The area of a circle

If we ask an uneducated man how to determine the area of a circle, he will not be able to give us the answer. However, if we use the formula ϖr^2, we can easily get the right answer. Every science subject has its own principles governing it. In the same manner, spirituality also has its own principles. *The laws of nature are the laws of spirituality.* Religion is pure science.

Why should we follow the laws of nature?

If we are studying in a school, we should follow the rules of the school. Similarly, if we are working in an office, we are bound to obey the rules laid down by the boss. We are a part of nature. Hence we must obey the laws of nature.

How are we a part of nature?

All things in nature (including man) are made up of cells. Just as the planets revolve round the sun, protons and electrons revolve round the nucleus in every cell of our body. Hence what is true of the universe, is true of our being. We are part of the cosmic universe. No matter how small or insignificant we may seem at times, we are always connected with the great whole. That should be the starting point of our thoughts and actions. Our body is made up of the five elements of nature. Therefore, we are part of nature. We are not apart from nature.

Birth is a composition of five elements in nature in a specific ratio. Death is the decomposition of the five elements. The body returns to nature.

The Universe

The whole universe is bound by certain laws. For example, all the planets move in a specific orbit at a specific speed. That is why, they do not collide with one another. Flowers bloom. Fruits ripen. Rain falls. Wind blows. All these occurrences are the result of the cosmic energy. It is an autonomous, natural energy. It is this energy that activates human beings also.

Spirituality, too, has laws

The law of spirituality is very simple. There is only one basic tenet: "Every good that we do, returns to us; and every evil that we commit will also return to us in the same ratio." Newton's third law, which says, "Every action has an equal and opposite reaction" can be seen in operation in all the incidents in our life. This law is applicable to all.

Some disbelieve

Some people do not believe this, because God does not punish wrong doers immediately. Certain plants like tomatoes, lady's fingers, beans etc., attain fruition very quickly. But coconut and palms take a long time to mature and bear fruit. In the same manner, some wrong deeds receive their punishment quickly; some take a long time. But they lie buried in our subconscious like seeds. This is called 'Cosmic record'. Mind is a recording machine. Even if we escape legal punishment, we can never escape punishment by nature.

56

Fate

Some people are eternal grumblers. They believe that God has frosaken them. They will say, god has deserted us; so we have deserted him. Some people will always complain that others have ruined their lives. No man can affect another man's destiny. Each one of us is master of his own fate. We carve our fate by the Karmic law of cause and effect.

Positive always overcomes the negative. This is the law of nature. Evil thoughts cannot stand before good thoughts. Courage overcomes fear. Patience overcomes anger. Love overcomes hatred. Purity overcomes lust. So let us nourish our mind with positive lofty thoughts. Let us be alert. Lord Jesus says "Watch and pray." We should live only to be a blessing to others by radiating joy, love and peace.

Vivekananda

Swami Vivekananda was once walking along in a forest. He saw a tiger approaching him. The tiger was about to pounce upon him. But he remained calm and fearless. The tiger looked at his face for some time and then retreated quietly. What we have to understand from this incident, is the fact that even animals will not harm a being who does not intend harm to them. This is a natural and scientific truth. The elements themselves wish to help a noble soul, not to harm him.

"By obeying Nature, we can control it."
—*Bacon.*

"If we go against Nature, it will not forgive us."
"Nature's laws are just."
—*Longfellow.*

Moses

It was by this same law (Nature's) that the sea laid out a path for Moses. Miracles performed by great saints, may be miracles to us, but not to them.

The power of the soul is limitless

The only difference between a saint and an ordinary man is that the saint never gives up. No matter how often he falls, he keeps on trying. He knows very well that the power of our soul is limitless.

"Those who win never quit;
Those who quit never win."

Religions

Religions that teach us these scientific truths and lead us on the right path, are indeed tools of science.

57

Way of life

The Indian way of life is based on ethics and spirituality. All our actions from dawn to dusk, are governed by scientific principles and hence are beneficial to the body and the mind. Let us see what they are,

Home:

People consider their homes as temples; and their daily duties as a form of worship. All their actions are dedicated to God. Such homes are indeed temples. Others are merely buildings.

Worship of the sun:

Salutations are offered to the Sun God at sunrise. Without the sun, the world cannot exist. There will be no greenery around. Hence we thank the sun for all his blessings. We also ask His pardon for all our lapses—committed knowingly or unknowingly. As we pray with our eyes closed, the sun's rays enter the eyes and stimulate the pituitary glands. The pituitary glands activate all the other glands. Hence, this worship enables the whole body to function properly and keep us healthy. Moreover, our skin derives vitamin D from the sunlight. The Sun is worshipped at sunset also.

Brushing the teeth:

Indians generally brush their teeth as soon as they get up in the morning. Drinking 'bed coffee' results in the 'descent' of the bacteria from the mouth to the stomach. This could cause diseases. Long before the toothbrush was invented by foreigners, Indians used neem twigs to brush their teeth.

Breakfast:

Most South Indians have idlis and a kind of chilli—dalpowder with gingelly oil, for breakfast. The urad dal used to make idlis, is rich in protein. Gingelly oil is also good for health. Wheat flour used for making puris and chappathis (by north Indians) is nutritious. During day, vegetables, milk, curds, greens and fruits are used.

Rice for crows:

Most families offer a little rice to the crows as soon as cooking is over. This is a sign of our care and concern for other living beings.

Kolam:

In South India, kolam or rangoli is an important ritual of daily life. Early in the morning, women wash the area in front of their houses and decorate it with intricate designs of rangoli. People of other countries are amazed at this practice. The presence of a kolam in front of a house lends it a special beauty. The pure air of the early morning, is good for women. The rice flour mixed with the chalk powder and used for drawing these kolams, becomes food for the ants. This is also an act of charity.

Greeting:

When Indians greet one another or their guests, they bring their palms together and wish their friends. This is a kind of acknowledgement of the fact that God dwells in every living being and hence must be respected. When people shake hands with one another, there is a risk of contracting diseases; whereas, if people greet one another with folded hands, there is no risk at all. North Indians greet one another by saying "Ram, Ram". Uttering God's names as often as we can, is a meritorious act that takes us closer to God. That is why the great Shivaji introduced this mode of greeting.

Before childbirth:

It is believed that a mother-to-be should have lofty thoughts and ideals. Only then, the child that is born will be worthy of his great lineage. Parents should also teach the child high morals and sound values.

The seventh month:

When a lady is seven months pregnant, a ritual is performed. All the relatives gather together and present many bangles to the lady.

There are two reasons for this. First, as these bangles move along the arm, they stimulate the acupuncture points and keep the lady healthy, so that childbirth is not difficult. Secondly, the tinkling sound made by the bangles is soothing and therefore conducive to the baby's health.

Tonsuring:

Children are usually tonsured before they complete one year. This is done to make the hair grow thicker and faster, so that even if children fall down, the head will be protected. This practice of tonsuring is celebrated in a grand manner. The maternal uncle has to hold the child in his lap. This serves to forge the bond between brothers and sisters.

The vermilion mark:

Indians, especially ladies, wear a vermilion mark on their forehead between the two eyebrows. This is a very sensitive spot which induces our thought processes. Our thoughts become purer. Also, it serves to ward off the evil eyes of the beholders. In addition, it enhances the beauty of the face.

Marriage:

During the marriage, the groom ties a 'thali' round the bride's neck. We can make out whether a lady is married or not, by the presence or absence of a thali round her neck. If a man is attracted by the beauty of a lady, he first looks at her neck. If he finds that she is married, he forgets her. This is Indian culture. During the marriage, the bride circumambulates the sacred fire in a clockwise by manner. This implies, that as the earth moves clockwise as ordained by nature, "I will also NOT do anything against nature". In India marriage is considered sacred. It is not a contract. A sacred fire is lit and sacred mantras are chanted. With God as witness, the groom says, "I shall be as chaste as Rama and I promise to live with you peacefully, procreating healthy intelligent off spring. I shall love you till I die. I will be true to you and I shall never separate myself from you." In return, the wife says, "I shall be unto you like Sita unto Rama. I shall serve thee till the end of my life in all sincerity. Thou art my very life. I shall realise God by serving thee as God." Feminine grace and modesty are the characteristics which adorn Indian ladies.

Family life:

Ladies play an important role in family life in India. God created a mother because He could not present Himself everywhere, says a proverb. Mothers in poor families would rather starve (themselves) and feed their children, than see them go hungry. Mothers lavish their love on their children. Those who have not received a mother's love in their childhood, are likely to become mentally disturbed when they reach adulthood. Some turn out to be anti-social elements. Men are prone to tension and stress as they go out, and have to meet different kinds of people and situations. But women are patient and calm because they remain at home.

Behind every successful man there is a lady, it is said. Lady is the power, the very soul of the home. Ladies strengthen the men and men become confident, creative and energetic which makes them prosperous. Life is sacred and home is considered to be a temple.

Parents:

Parents go to the temple to draw strength from the Deity and when they return home they maintain a similar vibration in which the children become wonderfully productive citizens. This brings peace on earth. Not a single village is deprived of temple. Ladies light an oil lamp in the morning and evening to bring the power of God and Devas into the home. This creates a happy and secured feeling and the family members escape from the pressures of daily life.

Joint family:

A unique feature of Indian culture, is the joint family system. Several families live in the same house, sharing their incomes, looking after the old and the infirm and practising tolerance, sacrifice, making minor adjustments and so on. This helps to develop noble qualities.

Ancestor Worship

Indians respect and tolerate elderly people. Their knowledge, their wisdom and their compassion guide the youngsters. We learn from their experience. It has become part of our culture.

Ancestor worship is performed on every death anniversary. Certain rites are performed and the favourite food of the departed soul is offered. Also auspicious days like new moon days are suitable for ancestor worship. The purpose of doing so is to express our gratitude even after their death and also to seek the blessings of our beloved ancestors.

One man, one women:

Chastity is the essence of Indian culture. Youngsters are taught to protect their chastity as a treasure. Expect his or her spouse all the others are treated only as brothers and sisters. Hence there is no risk of contracting diseases like AIDS.

Hospitality:

Showing hospitality to our guests is a feature of Indian culture.

Exercise:

Although scientific progress has popularised the use of the mixie, the grinder etc., in many households, there are women who still use the traditional stone grinder. This gives them exercise for the whole body. Wherever they want to go, people usually walk the distance. This prevents diseases like diabetes. When we walk, the kidneys function well. The cholesterol level comes down. Increase in the production of sweat results in the body getting rid of toxins and waste products.

The bed:

With the advance of civilisation, the practice of sleeping on soft beds has increased. Yet, there are people who spread a mat on the floor and sleep on it. Sleeping on a level surface prevents the bending of the backbone and the resultant backache. From ancient times people were aware that sleeping with your head towards the North was not good for health.

The role of festivals:

Many festivals are celebrated in India. The purpose of these festivals is, to make the common man communicate with God. During the festival, the presiding deity would be taken in a procession through the town or village. This enabled the old and the infirm to have 'darshan' or glimpse of the Lord, without having to go to the temple. The chariot carrying the deity is pulled by men from all walks of life, irrespective of their social, economic and educational status.

Epics:

Our epics tell us interesting tales. They also contain profound truths. In these epics God appears in human form and teaches us divine virtues.

Sprinkling of cowdung:

South Indians follow the custom of sprinkling diluted cowdung in front of their houses. This prevents germs and bacteria from entering the house.

Turmeric:

Women smear their bodies with turmeric everyday and then take their bath. This helps to destroy germs and increase one's immunity to diseases.

Manure:

There are innumerable chemical fertilizers today. It is believed that these fertilizers reduce the nutritive value of vegetables and fruits. Before the advent of such fertilizers, farmers used only natural wastes like cowdung, oilcake and dry leaves as manure. They were harmless to man and good for the plants.

The guest is God:

The Indians consider a guest as equal to God. The philosophy behind this, is that the guest is a representative of the whole human race. Every person born into this world, is under obligation to his parents, relatives, friends, teachers, townsmen, countrymen and to the whole human race scattered all over the globe.

For example, everyone who uses electrical lighting in the world, is under obligation to Thomas Alva Edison. To read a book published in a foreign country is to put oneself under obligation to all those workers who made the book possible, as well as to those who brought the book over land and sea to one's own town or city. How can one repay this obligation? Indians claim that the best solution to the problem is the practice of hospitality. The guest may be a person belonging to a different race, caste, religion or creed, but he must be treated with the greatest honour and generosity that is within one's power. It is only by catering to the needs of the guest or by charitable acts that the duties of a householder are considered to be complete.

The saree:

Women all over the world are attracted by the saree worn by Indian women. As a dress, it not only looks beautiful but serves to cover the whole body. Hence the beholders are prevented from entertaining evil thoughts about the wearer of the saree. On the contrary, she evokes a sort of respect for herself. She appears almost divine. Of course, one can wear the dress of one's choice. But it should be dignified.

58

Science in temples

Let us see how temples have been built on scientific bases. Temples are usually built in places where the magnetic force is very high. The pot shaped structures on top of the temple towers are made of bronze, which absorbs heat from the sun, so that the inside of the temple remains cool. This is conducive to the devotees who come to the temple to worship.

The Lingam in the sanctum sanctorum of the temple is cylindrical in shape. This symbolizes the universe which is cylindrical. To prevent the Lingam from falling, it is provided with a circular base.

Scientists have classified all objects in the universe under two heads: matter and energy. Our ancients had noted that Siva was matter and Shakthi was energy. Without matter there could be no energy. Hence our ancients envisaged the oneness of God and Goddess—Siva and Shakthi in the form of Ardhanareeswara.

As we sit in front of the Siva Lingam and meditate, the energy from the whole universe becomes available to us. However, our mind should be entirely free from any other thought to receive this energy. This is what Jesus implied, when he said, "Empty thyself and I shall occupy thee." Even 99% concentration is not enough. Only 100% concentration will work. Just as we get connected to the listener as soon as we dial a telephone number, we will be able to communicate with God as soon as we meditate earnestly. Meditation is like a bridge between us and God.

* Generally, people have a bath and with wet clothes on, they sit down to meditate. There is a scientific reason for this also. It is only when the body is moist, that it attracts electro-magnetic waves.

* In the temple compound there are various trees, like the neem, the bael and the pipal tree. The breeze wafted by the neem and the pipal trees is supposed to ward off several diseases, especially those affecting the womb. Basil leaves are capable of killing the germs in the stomach.

* The camphor and incense that are used in the temples during worship, are good for curing breathing problems. The rays from the burning camphor flame are good for the eyes. Mantras are chanted during worship in the temples. The vibrations emanating from the sound of these mantras help the mind to concentrate on God.

* The holy bath given to the idols is also beneficial. The smoke emanating from the 'yaga' spreads in all directions and destroys harmful germs. It nullifies the harmful effects of the pollution resulting from the smoke that is discharged by factories and vehicles, and safeguards our health. On realising these truths, an Athirudra Maha Yagam was conducted grandly in America recently for the

welfare of the whole world. Eighty seven veda experts from India were taken to America for the performance of this yaga.

About four thousand people from India, America, Canada and England participated in this yaga. The four vedas—Rig, Yajur, Sama and Adharvana—were chanted along with holy baths to the idols of worship.

59

Let us fall as seeds

7It may sometimes happen, that despite our enthusiasm and effort, we encounter defeat. At such times there is no need to despair. We should remember that in the universe, there is no such thing as an end. The so-called end of something is the beginning of something else. If God closes one door, He opens another. Hence, we should begin to work more resolutely, more enthusiastically and more skilfully. Even if we fall, let us fall as seeds, so that we rise again with greater vigour and freshness.

Goal

Have a vision; <u>work</u>; realise that vision

1   Realising our potential, we should decide whom we wish to emulate.
2   Hard work is needed to achieve this. Through meditation and good conduct we can increase our strength.

3 In the third stage we can realise our dreams.

Why the word 'work' has been underlined is because it is very important.

"You become what you wish to become", says the Gita. This is reiterated by Emerson, the great American philosopher. "A man is what he thinks he is." The Roman philosopher Marcus Aurelius says, "A man's life is what his thoughts make of it."

Work is religion. The Office should be our 'pooja' room. Let us work honestly and sincerely.

The God power within us is creative and when rightly called upon, can attract to us the conditions, circumstances and people we need to help us to attain something we have very much desired and have worked to achieve.

"Take up one idea. Make that one idea your life; think of it; dream of it; live on that idea. Let the brain, muscles, nerves, every part of your body be full of that idea and leave every other idea alone. This is the way to success."
—Swami Vivekananda.

"We can do anything we want to do
if we stick to it long enough."

Your desire must not be selfish

A point worth remembering, is that to succeed completely, your desires must not be selfish. Your ideas must go forth with the purpose of blessing or serving the world. The path of a complete circuit must be formed. If it is to benefit yourself exclusively, the circle or complete circuit is not formed and you may experience a short circuit in your life which may consist of certain limitations.

The changeless element

Everything in this world is liable to change. But one thing alone has remained unchanged since the world came into being. That is spirituality. Celebrities the world over, have always had an element of spirituality in them. Michael Jackson learnt yoga from Maharishi Mahesh Yogi. The great scientist Einstein was a spiritualist. The famous pop singer Madonna is also a spiritualist, and has released a pop album on spirituality. The heroine of the blockbuster film Titanic, came to India in quest of spirituality. Innumerable personalities like these, have won immortal fame and success through their spirituality. The younger generation should build its victories on the basis of spirituality.

Self management

Take the destiny of your life into your own hands; that is what self-management means. Each one of you is potentially infinite, says the Bhagavat Gita. Set your agenda. Draw your nourishment from your soul and in this manner you can handle your life and make it a pleasant experience, a celebration.

No matter what your religion is, be true to it.
If you are a Hindu, be a true Hindu.
If you are a Christian, be a true Christian.
If you are a Muslim, be a true Muslim.
Live you religion. That is what is important.

What do we leave behind?

Our forefathers in every country of the world, have left behind (for us) good traditions and a rich cultural heritage. What are we going to leave behind for the generations to follow? Should we not set a good example in our way of life? Is this not worth reflecting upon?

The greatest power on earth

All of us wish to progress in life. We all have dreams; we all have hopes. But we require immense power to realise our dreams. There is no doubt that God's power is the greatest on earth. If we wish to acquire such power, can it be done through ungodly acts? At times, (in our endeavour) we may experience depression and a sense of inability. But into God nothing is impossible. Let us pray that our life may become more and more worthy of His grace. And let His grace remove all our imperfections.

> *"Small things make perfection, but perfection is not a small thing."*

Spiritual socialism

Religion teaches us that the world is one. People are the same every where. Poor or rich, educated or uneducated, all are equal. Unfortunately however, people do not respect the street-sweepers or the grave-diggers. Yet, our civilization would be impossible without them. See others as an extension of your own self. See the universe as a unified whole and it will respond to you. This is called spiritual socialism. However rich a man is, and however high his position is, people will not recognize him as a great man. He who resides in people's hearts, can alone be considered worthy of occupying the throne befitting a king.

Readers would now have understood something of spirituality. Purity of mind is equal to spirituality. Nature does not change its regularity or orderliness. There is rhythm even in our heart-beats. What will happen if traffic rules are violated? If we are late by five minutes, we miss the train. How will a house look, if things are just strewn about in disorder? How will a song sound, if the tune and the rhythm are both wrong? There should be an order and discipline in everything. A vehicle without a brake is a dangerous thing. Similarly religion operates like a brake in our lives. I say this repeatedly: we have a long way to go and hence we have to regulate our efforts so that we may not go astray into the by-lanes, or fall into alluring pitfalls on the way.

Meaningless, celebrating the new millennium

As long as there are people who are illiterate in this world, as long as there are people who are poor in this world, as long as there are people who fight with one another because of their ignorance, there is no point in some people (who are lucky to have been blessed in every way) saying that we have progressed. Even if we have made great strides in science. we cannot call that real progress. Only when poverty and ignorance have been completely removed, can we say that we have progressed. Until then it is meaningless to celebrate the advent of the new millennium. All living beings have a heart beating in them. Animals care for their young as we do. Can man who possesses six senses, restrict his world only to himself and his family?

Let not evil grow

Only by removing ignorance can we eradicate evil. Suppose an injustice has been done and we remain indifferent (saying to ourselves that it does not concern us) then we are actually giving evil a chance to grow. Let us resolve to get rid of evil. It is better to light a candle than curse the darkness. With the light lit by each one of us, let us remove the darkness of ignorance. People's power is unlimited. Nothing is impossible in this world. It is high time we realise this. Whether it is an individual or a nation, the source of all strength is spirituality. Were it not for spirituality, we would have been exterminated by our own squabbles.

> *"Tryanny must withdraw before the tremendous power of moral strength."*
> —*Marshall*
> (in his Nobel Prize acceptance speech.)

Have we moved forward or backward?

Primitive man used stones and clubs to attack others. But we, with our superior intelligence, have only improved on his methods. We now threaten whole nations of people with atom bombs and military power. Have we moved forward or backward?

Fire cannot be quenched by fire. Terrorism cannot be quenched by organized terrorism. Let us meet problem at its root. The importance of religious books is more important now than ever before.

> *"If man will not put an end to war, war will put an end to mankind."*

Money

Ignorance and prejudice are only removed by knowledge. Money cannot buy a change of heart or a change of mind.

The great basic truth

Man has not recognized the great basic truth and principle that "To be free, you must first let others free."

Life is on earth seems to be fleeting and insecure. Atomic bombs can destroy our civilization, home, place of business and our self. The alarm bell has rung.

Intelligent force

A new intelligent force is needed in this world, the force of the human spirit. Could this human spirit be so liberated in the minds and hearts of men, it could free the world in an incredibly short time.

It is hightime we change this situation by the creative power of right thinking. There is no other choice for us now. *The 'creative power of thought' is more potent than governments and armies and atomic bombs.* The force of one thought can change the entire course of civilization, because thought comes from the mind and mind is born of soul which is unlimited because it is a part of God.

Thought travels with tremendous velocity through space. Thought has weight, shape, size, form and colour. It is a dynamic force. A wrong thought binds. A right thought liberates. Therefore let us think rightly and attain freedom.

William James, the father of American psychology, said that thought has the power to move the world.

"Peace hath her victories
No less renowned than war."

The world cannot change until we change

As we gain an understanding of the universal laws activating us, we can see that we are actually creating the world in which we live. The world, therefore, cannot change until we change.

Non-violence

In the Bible is a story of people who brought to Christ a woman who had sinned. The people wanted her to be stoned to death. But Christ said, "He that is without sin among you, let him first cast a stone at her". No one could condemn her and Jesus said, "Neither do I condemn you. Go, and sin no more". Jesus Christ demonstrates non-violence of the brave.

Prophet Mohammed was sitting with his friend Abu Bhakkar when a man came up and shouted at him. Abu listened for awhile and then reacted angrily. Immediately Mohammed left. When Abu complained that Mohammed did not stand by him in his time of need, he replied, "When you kept silent, I understood that you sought help from God and I realised God's presence. When you shouted, I realised that God was not present and you were handling the problem yourself. I decided that where God was not present neither would I be".

You are the light of the world

Youngsters! You are the ones who are going to brighten the 21st century. Yes. *You are the light of the world.* This moment you have resolved to become good. Your victory too, has become a foregone conclusion.

Revolt

What we now need is a change. To effect a change, a revolution is necessary. But the revolution that we are going to initiate is a very simple one. It is a spiritual revolution. It is a revolution that will make people good. Other revolutions involve the use of weapons. We don't need weapons. Our only weapon is love. Let us usher in a new chapter.

The goal is set

Our mind is fixed; our goal is set, and we will not give up come what may. Never mind how many times we fall; we'll keep on trying. Even if we fail and everything around us is crumbling, let us hold fast to our faith in God. Let us lift ourselves by the bootstraps and keep on trying. If we can do this, we will find ourselves protected and guided at every moment, because we know that God is all-loving and all-protecting.

"When everything is lost, remember the future remains."

Statue

If an ordinary stone has to be transformed into a beautiful statue, it has to be chiselled. Gold has to be melted and beaten if it has to be shaped according to our wishes. A diamond will glitter only if it is polished again and again. So why not we take a little extra trouble? Remember Rome was not built in a day. Let us gather all our a efforts to reach our goal.

Chain

Humanity, like a great chain, is actually as strong as its weakest link. The weakest link, if not strengthened by humanity as a whole, will eventually break and bring the entire civilization down.

Ordinary person

Youngsters! Do you ever feel, "What can I do? What difference can I make? I am just an ordinary person." No, no. You are the image of God. Every person who believes in God and goodness, makes a difference. Those who have read this book are no longer ordinary. You are extra-ordinary. You have unlimited power, because you have united yourself with the basic power of the universe.

Remember

God is everywhere. Hence, we are always in His presence. He knows what we think, say and do. We are surrounded by an ocean of cosmic energy. We do not feel any weakness, because we know that an infinite ocean of strength is flowing into us as long as we keep the channel open. We do not want to take from others, because we know that there are infinite possessions within us.

The beginning and the end

We have not time to rest. Let us walk the path of righteousness now. A good beginning can only have a good ending. Even tomorrow may be too late. It is said that a thing well begun is a thing half done.

"Winning starts with beginning and
Beginning starts with a single action."

60

Let us take a pledge

Let us take a pledge that within a year we shall change the whole world. Let every one of us take pledge, "To wipe every tear from every eye". Think of a society "Where the mind is without fear, where the head is held high and where knowledge is free."

Brothers and sisters, let us go back to the first chapter of this book. Let us celebrate 'Raksha Bandhan' all over the world. An ideal life is a life full of ideals. Our ideals must be truly noble. If we are to solve the problems of the world, people of the world should be united. Let us not be separated by narrow geographical boundaries. Only through unity can problems be solved. There is no doubt about this, because we are the image of God; nay, we are God ourselves!

An intelligent force is needed, now. Everyone who reads this book is invited to work with me to wipe out the darkness of ignorance and make the 21st century a bright one.

Yes. You are the light of the world.

Personality

Name, fame and prosperity—we may have all these in abundance; but they cannot make our life complete. And until that is done, we shall strive in vain for stability. Whichever course of life we follow, it should be guided by the light of spirituality. That alone will make life stable, complete and successful. There can be no painting without a canvas. We should be physically healthy. There should be room in our life for play and exercise. (not watching the TV all the time). More than anything else, we should be able to charm others with our good qualities and magnetic personality. Life, honour and noble qualities blossom and attain fruition only in one whose conduct and behaviour are good. Always be cheerful. Realise the magnetic power of divine love and bless all the world.

Work for it

Enough of words! I have given you all the details relevant for a useful and good life. It is up to you to put all that into practice. You can't get money by watching someone else work. You have to work for it yourself. Similarly you must make maximum effort now to reach your goal. Then you will see that your life—every minute of it-becomes a magic existence! Do not worry if you don't make instant progress. It is all a matter of time. Every caterpillar will become a butterfly. It is just a matter of time!

> *"Whatever you can do, or dream, you can begin it.*
> *Boldness has genius, power and magic in it."*
> —*Goethe.*

Golden sayings

"Look into your heart. That is where God resides."
—*Prophet Mohamed*

"Good conduct is a great river. Good
habits are its tributaries."
—*Martin*

"Happiness can only result from good conduct."
—*Samuel Taylor Coleridege*

"He who quakes at minor disturbances,
can never achieve great things.
He who cheats others, cheats himself first."
—*Italian proverb*

"Good education is nation's greatest defence."
—*Edmund Burke*

"Good men are shaped only by mothers.
The future of a society is in the hands of its mothers.
Forget the periods of adversity in your life. But
don't forget the lessons it taught you."
—*Alphonia*

"One of the duties of every man, is service to others."
— *Tolstoy*

"Merely dipping one's body in water is not a bath. He alone is clean whose mind is pure."
— *Dharma Sastra*

"Poverty, disease and other misfortunes are the fruits of the tree of one's own deeds."
— *Dharma Sastra*

"He who refuses to think of progress will be left behind."
— *Goethe*

"Be a leader. Or be with leader. You will become great."
— *Dr. V.N. Peel*

"An enthusiast will not be afraid of opposition. On the contrary, he will be inspired to work harder and achieve success."
— *Hitler.*

"Do not despair. You are not far from success. Move forward with confidence."
— *Rutherford*

"There is a force which cannot be suppressed by any other force on earth. It is man's mental power."
— *Carlyle*

"He who wishes to serve people truly
will inspire a thousand idealists."
—*Mahatma Gandhi*

"Leave your burden to Christ. He will take care
of you. He will not let the just stumble."
—*The Bible*

"An evil policy is worse than fire."
—*Avvaiyar*

"Comforting the sick is the greatest
help one can give them."
—*Mother Teresa*

"He who feeds a hungry man is like God."
—*Gandhi*

"Though vast, sea water cannot be used for
drinking. Water from a small spring is good to
drink. Do not assess anybody by his size.
Valour is not of the body. It is of the mind."
—*Gandhi*

"He who is industrious will have a blanket.
Lazy people will have only sheep."
—*An Entonian proverb*

"It is not the rivers alone that empty themselves into
sea. In our country people's power is also wasted."
—*Swami Vivekananda*

"If you cannot honour your parents who are the living gods, how will you worship an invisible God?"
—*Swami Vivekananda*

"If every individual progresses, the nation will certainly progress. When spirituality loses its hold on man, it signals the downfall of society."
—*Swami Vivekananda*

"A nation's progress is measured by its people's education and conduct."
—*Swami Vivekananda*

"Three factors contribute to success. They are purity of mind, faith and perseverence."
—*Swami Vivekananda*

"A bad thought is the most dangerous of all thieves."

"An army of sheep led by a lion would defeat an army of lions led by a sheep."

"While others wondered, feared, hoped and prayed, the real leader comes forward to rally the people and tell them what to do."

"The best things in life are free."

"Forewarned is forearmed."

"Things done cannot be undone."

"If you lie down with dogs, You'll get up with fleas."

"When money starts to speak truth becomes silent."

"When everything is lost, remember the future remains."

"It is better to understand a little than to misunderstand a lot."

"If man will not put an end to war, war will put an end to mankind."

"The happiest people do not have the best of everything. They just make the best of everything".

"Just as mountains have valleys and peaks, life also has got its own share of ups and downs, and successes and failures. It is foolish to say that I would enjoy only the peaks and not the valleys. The wise and the strong look at the scenic beauty of both".

"If you want peace of mind, do not find fault with others. Rather see your own faults. Learn to make the whole world your own. Look for merits".

"An individual working by himself can only achieve limited results. It is only when individuals work together as a team that remarkable results can be achieved".

T—Together
E—Everyone
A—Achieves
M—More

"Positive people laugh to forget and negative people forget to laugh".

"Good humor is the oil for the wheels of life, without which there is more noise and more friction".

"There are two types of people, the first type 'who brings happiness wherever they go' and second type 'who brings happiness whenever they go'".

"The first sign that you are becoming religious is that you are becoming cheerful. By being pleasant and smiling, it takes you nearer to God, nearer than any prayer".

"Just as a computer works on what kind of software has been installed in it, so too a child's personality is only an expression of what kind of mental impression have been inculcated in it".

"Everyone can play the role of a master, but it is very difficult to be a servant".

"No power in the universe can withhold from anyone, anything he really deserves".

"Great things are done only by great sacrifices".

"Whenever you are in distress, just say to yourself, God is with me. What fear need we have?"

"You can lead a horse to water, but you can't make it drink. Books and teachers can only point out the way—it is up to us to practice, if we really wish to change".

"Practice makes us what we shall be".

"Discipline is the bridge between goals and accomplishment. A self disciplined person is always successful".

"All actions good or bad arise first in the mind. Fill the mind with highest thoughts. Go on doing good. Thought is at the bottom of all progress, of all success or failure".

"Each work has to pass through these stages-ridicule, opposition and then acceptance".

"Men are more valuable than all the wealth of the world".

"Kindness and love can buy you the whole world; lectures, books and philosophy—all these stand lower than these".

"The sign of life is strength and growth. Every idea that strengthness must be taken up and every thought that weakens must be rejected".

"Can a leader be made? A leader is born. First by birth, and secondly unselfish that's a leader".

"Use agreeable and wholesome language towards even the greatest enemy".

"He who is the servant of all is their true master. He whose love knows no end, has the whole world lying at his feet".

"Organization is power and the secret of it is obedience".

"Unless you are simple, you cannot know God, the Simple One".

"To be unselfish is to be able to sacrifice and renounce one's petty comforts and pleasures for the sake of a higher good".

"All our actions must be it small or large, must b performed in a spirit of worship. If a man is called to be a street sweeper he should sweep streets even as Michelangelo painted or Shakespeare wrote poetry. He should sweep streets so well that all the hosts of heaven and earth will pause to say "Here lived a great sweeper who did his job well".

"Watch a man do his most common actions; those are indeed the things which will tell you the real character of a great man. He alone is the really great man whose character is great always the same wherever he be".

"The steam has to be controlled and then redirected into a steam engine to pull the locomotive. Similarly to direct the forces of the body and mind by control to even the smallest task is the secret of success".

"A controlled mind is one's greatest friend and an uncontrolled mind is one's greatest enemy".

"The greater the responsibilities one under takes, the greater the privileges one enjoys. Privilages come to him unsought. Privilages and reaponsibilities always go hand in hand".

"No tree eats its own fruit. It strives to produce the fruit and gives it up for the use of others. The highest and purest form of work culture is to give, serve and save all, all the time at every level".

"From anger results delusion, from delusion results confusion of memory, from confusion of memory results destruction of intelligence, and from destruction of intelligent he perishes".

"A tortoise when threatened, immediately withdraws all its limbs(feet, head and tail) into a shell, thus protecting itself from external harm. We too must be similarly able to withdraw our senses from sense—objects to preserve emotional stability in the face of temptation and provocation".

"Man is great and superior to animals only because of his faculty of discrimination. Whenever a man falls or suffers, it is due to loss of this power of discrimination".

"Oils and metals are available in the bowels of earth. But they are to be drilled, processed and purified before they are made usable. So also man to be of use has to undergo the process of purification through meditation".

"God is the great universal master of music, who composes and directs the cosmic orchestra of infinite dimensions. It is he who makes everyone speak, hear and move according to his tunes. When our life gets attuned to God's song, our life too becomes a divine life".

"A cashier working in a bank, who has to handle a lot of cash, knows that he is not the owner or the enjoyer of that sum, because it is owned and enjoyed by the bank. He is only entrusted a work which he should do earnestly and honestly. So also, if we feel that this world is God's creation, and He is in the heart of everyone, making them do as they do, then we would feel that he is the doer and that the results of our actions are also His. We would then become free from ego and possessiveness".

"Good education is an ability to understand life. It should be man making".

"One has to pray for the good of all, for the good of whole humanity. This kind of universal prayer expands our consciousness and loosens all selfish knots".

"A person established in truth cannot utter a falsehood even by mistake".

"A person established in non-violence has no enemies".